Anatomy of Dressage

By H. Schusdziarra and V. Schusdziarra

Translated from the German
by Cynthia Hodges, M.A.
Edited by Reina Abelshauser

Co-published by

The United States Dressage Federation, Inc.
Lexington, Kentucky

and

Half Halt Press, Inc.
Boonsboro, Maryland

The Anatomy of Dressage
Translation © 2004 by Half Halt Press, Inc.

First published in Germany as *Gymmnasium des Reiters* by
Heinrich Schusdziarra and Volker Schusdziarra

© 1994 by Müller Rüschlikon Verlags AG, CH-6330 Cham. First
published in 1978 by Verlag Paul Parey, Berlin & Hamburg.

Translated from the German by Cynthia Hodges, M.A.
Edited by Reina Abelshauser
Cover photo courtesy of Bob Tarr, www.bobtarr.com
Cover design by Design Point, Eppng, NH

Co-published by the United States Dressage Federation,
220 Lexington Green Circle, Suite 510, Lexington, KY 40503 and
Half Halt Press, Inc., P.O. Box 67, Boonsboro, MD 21713.

Library of Congress Cataloging-in-Publication Data
    Schusdziarra, Heinrich.
    [Gymnasium des Reiters. English]
    Anatomy of dressage / by H. Schusdziarra and V. Schusdziarra ; translated from the
    German by Cynthia Hodges ; edited by Reina Abelshauser.
        p. cm.
        ISBN 0-939481-69-3 (pbk)
        1. Dressage. 2. Human anatomy. I. Schusdziarra, Volker. II. Abelshauser, Reina. **III.**
    Title.
SF309.5S4313 2004 798.2'3—dc22

2004054083

Anatomy of Dressage

Table of Contents

Foreword   7

Introduction   9

Part One: Anatomy   13

  Bones and Ligaments   15

      The Spine   15

      The Pelvis, Thigh, and Hip Joint   19

      The Hip Joint Ligament   27

  Muscles   32

      Muscles of the Seat   32

      Muscles of the Thigh and Lower Leg   33

      Abdominal Muscles   40

      Back Muscles   42

Part Two: The Requirements of Riding from an Anatomical Perspective   45

      The Seat: Resting on Three Points of Support?   47

      Bracing the Lower Back   48

      Using the Leg   54

      Going with the Motion of the Horse   58

      Half Halts and Full Halts   66

      Balance—Going with the Motion of the Horse   74

      Suppleness and Gripping   80

      The Chair Seat and the Hollow Back   83

      The Use of the Seat Muscles   87

      The Spiral Seat   87

      Riding Through the Corner   98

      Shoulder-In and Half Pass   100

      The Transition to Canter   102

Part Three: Training   105
Part Four: Teaching and Learning   123

Bibliography   141
Illustrations   142
Index   143

FOREWORD

An elderly doctor who had read Müseler's *Riding Logic* for the first time about 50 years ago recommended that classic to a young medical student a few years ago: his son. Because they had the good fortune of being able to ride together, there were frequent discussions concerning the sport, especially about dressage. They did not always share the same opinion and finally decided on human anatomy to act as an arbitrator to settle the disputes they had. They thought it advisable to share the impartial arbitrator's very objective and fair judgment, as well as the conclusions that could be drawn from it. We took on this task in appreciation for the years we spent riding together.

In order to make the necessary anatomical fundamentals comprehensible to laypeople, appropriate illustrations were needed. Mr. Roland Helmus has provided exceptionally good and impressive drawings. For this we give him our special thanks.

Dr. Heinrich Schusdziarra, M.D.
Dr. Volder Schusdziarra, M.D.

Stapelfeld, Summer 1978

INTRODUCTION

Riding as a sport has become ever more popular over the last few years. The number of riding organizations has increased, as has the number of their members. To the same degree, the number of participants at horse shows is also growing, and young rider's interest in dressage also seems to be increasing. Through the organizations, they receive instruction, and those who are especially interested have the appropriate books at home so they can supplement the exercises they learn in the lesson with theory.

The rider who has worked hard in the riding lesson, but who has not been able to accomplish the desired exercises either to his or to his trainer's satisfaction, later ponders the lack of success of the desired exercises. At home, he looks to the riding manuals by Müseler, for example, which he definitely does not do for the first time. Once in a while, he will concentrate on individual parts to figure out why one required exercise or another was so difficult. With new resolve, he goes to the next lesson, but success in dressage does not happen that quickly.

Is it possible that Müseler's riding manual is not enough? There are others. Let us look at what Podhajsky has to say. In addition, there are Wätjen, Bürger, Steinbrecht and others. These great dressage riders and instructors have written good books. In most of them, however, there is more about training the horse than training the rider. Even after intense study of the sections about training the rider, the practical question remain:, "How do you do it?" How do you, for example, halt the horse or brace your back? What do you have to do, and how do you do it?

The rider will not find a satisfactory answer to these questions in the riding manuals. We do not in any way wish to write a new riding manual. Better riders and instructors with great riding ability and rich practical experience are called upon to take on that task. We are making an attempt here to supplement the available riding manuals, to make them more understandable through the approach of anatomical function. We will explain the movements and how the muscles are used to perform them in order to answer the question, "How do you do that?"

To that end, we must impart knowledge about the anatomy, because without it, an explanation of the appropriate use of the individual limbs, and an explanation of the movements associated with them, is not possible. Without it, it is not possible to talk about appropriate instruction and training methods. Without an understanding of anatomy, the student will not understand the instructions. He will not be in the position to perform specific movements at will or to judge the correctness of his performance.

Therefore, we found it necessary to place a certain amount of descriptive anatomy at the beginning of our book. It was difficult for us to decide how comprehensive that should be. The more detailed and more in depth we describe it, the more difficult our book would be for those who have no medical or anatomical training. Because we have to assume that most riders and readers are laypeople, we have kept the anatomical descriptions limited to what is necessary to explain the movements made during riding. From the sical perspective, we will be able to discuss the individual requirements of riding theory.

Although our book is at times critical, nothing derogatory is intended toward the riding manuals or about the riding instructors mentioned.

PART ONE

Anatomy

BONES AND LIGAMENTS

THE SPINE

In our discussion of the spine, we will refer to Figure 1. This lateral view shows the characteristic curvatures of the human spine especially well. In the area of the cervical spine and lumbar spine is the lordosis, which curves toward the front. In the area of the thoracic spine is the kyphosis, which curves toward the back. The two lordosic sections are the more flexible.

These curvatures have, of course, their reason and purpose. They make it possible for the spine to act as a load-bearing spring. This construction plays a highly important role in stabilizing the torso in the upright position. It enables, the spine to give like a spring when burdened in the vertical position, which greatly increases its load-bearing ability.

The disks between the vertebrae, which are easy to recognize on the figure between the individual vertebrae, and which contain a gelatinous core, play an important role in the springiness while in the upright position. They act like the buffers on railroad cars. Without these spring elements, every jolt that occurs at the bottom of the spine would continue unimpeded up the spine and at full strength, and would eventually affect the head and the brain. Depending on the strength of the jolt, discomfort, pain, injuries or harm would result, due to compression, concussions or to fractures of the spine. The impact is broken at the curved sections of the spine.

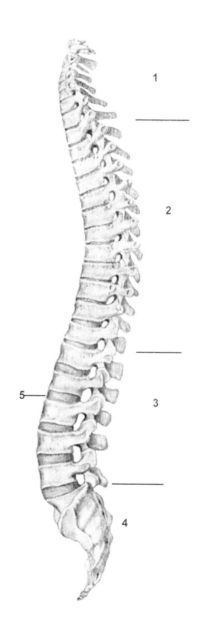

FIGURE 1. Spinal
Column—Lateral View

*1. cervical vertebrae;
2. thoracic spine;   3. lumbar spine;   4. sacrum;
5. intervertebral disk*

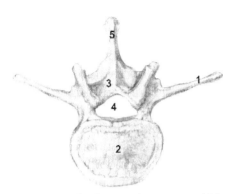

FIGURE 2. Single Vertebra—Dorsal View

1. transverse process; 2. vertebral body; 3. lamina;
4. spinal canal;
5. spinous process

Because the spine has more than one curve to it, the effect of the pressure and impact is distributed even more.

In Figure 2, we see a vertebra depicted with the oval vertebra and the vertebral curve, from which the spinous process and transverse processes emanate. The muscles are attached to them. The vertebral bodies and transverse processes enclose an opening. The vertebral openings lie exact-

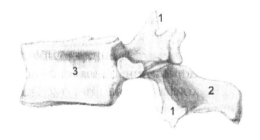

FIGURE 3. Single Vertebra - Lateral View

1. joint surfaces; 2. spinous process; 3. vertebral body

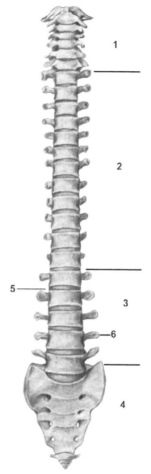

FIGURE 4. Spine - Frontal View

1. cervical spine; 2. thoracic spine;
3. lumbar spine; 4. sacrum;
5. intervertebral disk;
6. transverse process.

ly one on top of the other and form a channel through which the spinal cord runs.

In Figure 3, we see a lateral view of the joint surfaces of a single vertebra. The joint connections to the neighboring vertebra are made with sinuous capsules and ligaments. In this way, the spine becomes a rod that is divided into sections and that is able to move in any direction, including sideways.

Figure 4 shows us the spine from a frontal view, in which it appears completely straight. Sideways curvatures, that is, those that would be easily seen from this perspective, should normally not be present. If they are detected, they are abnormal. If they do not occur to a great extent, they usually do not cause any problems. However, they do disturb the symmetry of the body and, in this way, can be noticeably troublesome and restrictive when using the spine in special ways, for example, while riding.

At the lower end of the spine we see in Figure 4 the sacrum, which does not consist of individual vertebrae. The sacral vertebrae have grown into a single bone, which, as Figure 1 shows tips backward underneath the fifth lumbar vertebra. This transition from the lumbar spine to the sacrum is especially important, because here the movement of the entire spine acts against the movement of the entire pelvis. The last disk and the joints between the fifth lumbar vertebra and the sacrum are adapted especially for this. The rider should pay special attention to the term "small of the back," because it refers to an important anatomical region for the dressage rider.

THE PELVIS, THIGH, AND HIP JOINT

With Figure 5, we will now explain the individual parts of the pelvis and its anatomical connections that are necessary for further understanding.

At the rear side of the pelvis, we have the sacrum as we just learned about in the discussion of the spine. Connected to the sacrum on either side are the two iliac

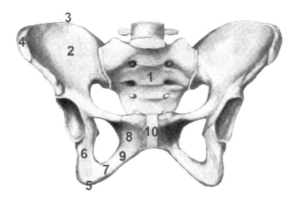

FIGURE 5. The Pelvis

1. sacrum; 2. ilium; 3. iliac crest; 4. anterior superior iliac spine
5. ischial tuberosity; 6. superior ischial ramus; 7. inferior ischial ramus
8. superior pubic ramus; 9. inferior pubic ramus; 10. pubic crest.

bones, next to which we want to note the iliums, the iliac crest, and the anterior superior iliac spine. Underneath those, we have the ischium, the ischial tuberosity, and the superior and inferior ischial ramus. They merge into the front to form the superior and inferior pubic ramus. In the pubic crest—you can feel it in the front toward the bottom of the abdominal wall—the two pubic bones are joined on either side.

In this way, the pelvic bones and the sacrum form a self-contained, fixed ring whose individual parts cannot be moved separately from each other. Therefore, it is impossible for us to move or tense our sacrum in an isolated manner. Every movement or change in position is always connected to a movement or a change in position of the entire bony pelvic ring.

This fact is of such fundamental meaning to our further thoughts and discussion that we must refer back to it repeatedly.

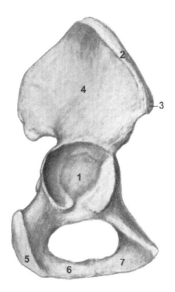

FIGURE 6. The Exterior of the Pelvis

1. cetabulum; 2. iliac crest; 3. anterior superior iliac spine; 4. ilium
5. ischial tuberosity; 6. inferior ramus of schium;
7. inferior pubic ramus.

Figure 6 shows the exterior of the pelvis where the iliac bone, ischium and pubic bone come together to form the acetabulum. It resembles the hollow part of half of a sphere and is made up of cartilage. The ball-like head of the thigh bone fits into this joint.

The spherical head of the hip joint, which is shown in Figure 7, fits exactly into the articular cavity.

In Figure 8, we see, as indicated by arrows, how the weight of the entire body is supported by the pelvis by means of both hip joints.

Here we would like to interrupt our description of the anatomy and talk about the process of movement that occurs in our hip joints when we tilt our pelvis forward backward

FIGURE 7. The Thigh Bone

*1. femoral head; 2. femoral neck; 3. femur-
al shaft; 4. knee joint*

while standing. We want to address it now, while the anatomical description of the pelvis is still fresh in our minds. The
description of this movement is important because we will
need it later to explain the bracing of the back.

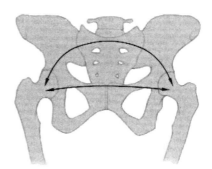

FIGURE 8.
Weight Distribution on the Hip
Joints in a Standing Position

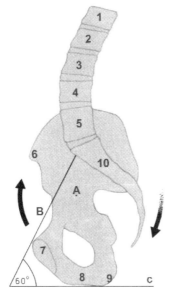

FIGURE 9. Lateral View of the
Pelvis, Normal Position, Seen
From the Inside

*1–5. lumbar vertebrae; 6. anterior
superior iliac spine; 7. pubic
crest; 8. superior ischial ramus and
pubis; 9. ischial tuberosity;
10. sacrum*

Imagine a line going across the pelvis and both hip joints. In Figure 9, we can see a lateral inner view of one half of the pelvis and the lumbar spine. Point A represents the aforementioned line.

The pelvis is in the normal position when the person is standing. We see the lumbar spine that curves toward the front and the sacrum that tips backward. The entire pelvis ring is included in this tilted position of the sacrum because they are connected. We can illustrate this more clearly if we draw Line B from the upper end of the sacrum to the front through the pubic crest, which, as it runs forward and down, forms an angle of 60 degrees with Line C, which runs underneath the pelvis.

The arrows outside of the pelvis show the direction in which the pelvis tilts around Axis A. We see the result of this tilt in Figure 10. The sacrum and the rear part of the pelvic ring

FIGURE 10. Lateral View of
the Pelvis, Pelvis Tipped to
Rear, Seen From the Inside

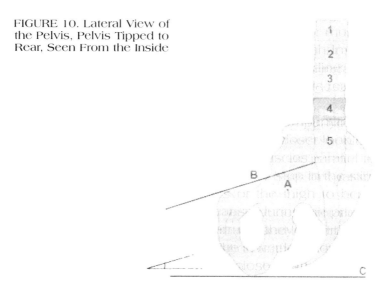

have lowered and have moved from their backward tilted position to a more perpendicular position. Since the pelvic ring is not flexible, its front part had to be raised to the same degree as the rear part was lowered. Line B clearly shows the degree of lifting. Its angle down is much less steep, and the angle formed with horizontal C has become considerably smaller.

How does this pelvic tilt play out when we are sitting in the saddle? The pelvis is tilted around the same axis that runs at a slant through it and the hip joints. The weight distribution has changed, however. Here, we must compare Figures 8 to 11. While the weight of the body is supported by the hip joints while standing, when sitting it rests on the ramuses of ischium and pubis as the arrows in Figure 11 show. In this instance the tilt affects these bones.

Now place your hand under your seat. It will not be difficult to feel the ischial tuberosities that are set the farthest back. From there, feel forward at an angle over the inferior ischial ramus to the end of the inferior pubic ramus. If you find this difficult while standing, assume an easy squatting position. You will be able to feel the entire head of the bone and also notice that it is slightly curved like a round container. If you move your pelvis while feeling the head of the bone or when you rise out of the squatting position, you can feel how the ischial tuberosities and the head of the bone of the ramus of ischium and pubis move. Depending on the size of your body, it is 2–3 inches (6–8 cm long) and symmetrically positioned on both sides. This is the bony foundation for the rider's seat. Upon these bones your pelvis moves when tilted in the previously shown manner.

FIGURE 11. Weight Distribution Through the Pelvis with Body in Sitting Position.

Figures 5–11 confirm what you felt:Tthe heads of the bone of the ramus of ischium and pubis are not straight but, rather, rounded. Therefore, they can never rest their entire length on the saddle. Depending on the degree of curvature, a more or less large section of the arc will serve as the foundation of the seat. Compare that to the rockers on a rocking chair. Here, too, the weight rests, depending on the degree of curvature of the rocker, always on a more or less great but limited section of the rockers. With the tipping of the chair to the front or back, the weight-bearing section rolls more on the front or back part of the rocker. We reach the most extreme position of this pelvic tilt to the back when we roll the pelvis on the rockers so far back that we sit only on the two Ischial tuberosities.

The comparison with the rocking chair is only meant to clarify the way the pelvis tips to the front and back, and rolls on the ramuses of ischium and pubis. Because there is a considerable size difference between the rockers of a rocking chair and the approximately 6 cm long rockers of the ramuses of ischium and pubis, the scope of movement is different, too.

There is another difference in the rocking chair, which you already might have noticed if you looked closely at the pelvis in Figure 5. The rocker ends of a rocking chair remain at the same distance from each other in the front and back. The rockers of the ramuses of ischium and pubis at their hindmost parts, the two pin ischial tuberosities, are farthest apart. They come together in the front, so that they unite at the pubic bone. Both constructions have their justification depending on their intended use. The lower frame of the rocking chair must be built like that because it is designed to only tip forward and backward. The lower frame of our pelvis must be constructed differently for dressage riding, because the tipping motion that was just illustrated is only one of the pelvic movements that must be made while riding dressage. A sideways tipping or a combination of a sideways tilting and turn-

ing of the pelvis will be necessary as well. These requirements can explain the rockers of the ramuses of ischium and
pubis by the way they function.

THE HIP JOINT LIGAMENT

In this section, we want to proceed as we did in the
previous one. From the great number of tendons and ligaments in the area of the pelvis and hip joint, we will only talk
about the one we consider to be important.

The hip joint ligament strengthens the thick joint cap-
sule of the hip joint on its front side. We see on Figure 12 that
it goes from the edge of the articular cavity in the area of the
iliac bone to the femoral neck of the hip. Therefore, it is called
the iliofemoral ligament. If we occasionally use Latin names,
then it will only happen once in order to clarify which of the
hip joint ligaments we mean in this case. Afterwards we will
go back to a more common term. The ligament that is important to us we will call the hip joint ligament in our further discussion for the sake of simplicity.

Now let's take another look at Figure 12. It is clear that
the fibers of the ligament run in the shape of a screw. In the
vertical position of the hip, which is shown here, they are
tightly wound. When examining the ligament closer, you will
see that this peculiar fiber structure makes it possible to lift the
leg forward and up. This is because the ligament is more
relaxed and becomes looser the more the leg is lifted from the
hip joint. It does not allow the leg to be lifted farther to the
back from the hip in the vertical hanging position because in
this leg position the ligament is already twisted to the utmost
due to the pattern of the fibers.

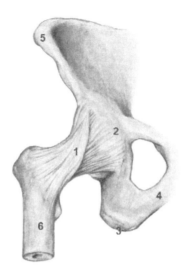

FIGURE 12.
1. hip joint ligament;   2. edge of hip socket;   3. ischial tuberosity;
4. ischial-pubic ramus;   5. front superior iliac spine;   6. thigh bone

You may stop and say, "Something does not sound right. I can also lift my leg backward while standing." You stand up, try it, and see that the leg can also be lifted back. That is possible, but not in the hip joint! An illusion creeps in easily here. The ligament blocks the hip joint in its vertical position of the hip because of the fibers' pattern. If the hip, despite this, is lifted farther back, the blocking ligament of the pelvis tips forward, and with the pelvis tipped forward, the hip moves backward. You can test this if you place a hand on the upper part of your iliac spine on the front edge of the iliac crest. Where is that, you may ask? When one heeds the command in gymnastics, "Put your hands on your hips," the index finger is right on it. You can also see it in Figures 5, 6, 12 and 13. This iliac spine stays still if you lift the leg forward and then let it fall back to the vertical position. If, however, you raise your leg farther backward from a standing position, the iliac spine begins to tilt forward. This is a sign that lifting the leg farther backward from a standing position is only indirectly possible because the pelvis tips forward over the hip ligament.

The point of this exercise was to help you feel how the hip and pelvis take on a mutual dependence of motion via the hip ligament. Now that you have felt this movement, it may become even clearer if we look at it again in Figures 13 a–c in our further discussion.

We want to know which role the hip ligament plays in riding. Keep in mind that we have already discussed the pelvic motion, its tipping forward and backward on pages 21 to 26. When we sit normally, for example, regardless of whether sitting in a chair or in the saddle, the weight of the body rests on the two pin bones, and the thigh is lifted forward 90 degrees. The pelvis is tipped backward to the greatest degree and the hip ligament is totally relaxed (Figure 13 a).

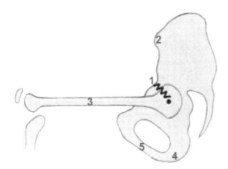

FIGURE 13a. Hip Joint Ligament Relaxed in Sitting Position

1. hip joint ligament; 2. anterior superior iliac spine; 3. thigh bone; 4. ischial tuberosity; 5. ischial-pubic ramus

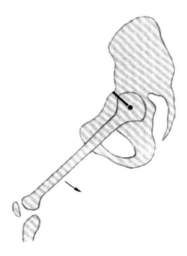

FIGURE 13b. Hip Joint Ligament Flexed After Lowering the Thigh

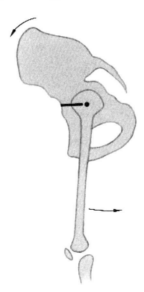

FIGURE 13c. Flexed Hip Joint Ligament Tilts the Pelvis Forward When Thigh is Lowered More

With the foundation of our seat arranged like this, we remain sitting on the pin bones with our the legs hanging on either side while sitting in our saddle, but while standing we cannot do this to such an extent that the thighs reach the vertical position. Before this can happen, the blocking effect of the ligament comes into play. The causes for this are the inwardly turned thighs and the spiral pattern of the ligament. With this, we reach the condition as shown in Figure 13b.

The ligament is tensed, but the rider's knee is not positioned deep enough yet. The thigh must be positioned farther down and back. Because the tight, sinewy ligament does not give one millimeter, the thigh can only be lowered if the ligament tips the pelvis forward, as you felt earlier. When this happens, the foundation of the seat rolls from the pin bones to the ramus of ischium and pelvis (Figure 13c).

From this, we can conclude that the following are mutually exclusive: a rider's seat resting way back on the two ischial tuberosities and a thigh position that is as close as possible to the vertical in order to attain as deep a knee position as possible. A deep knee is only possible when the pelvis rolls from the ischial tuberosities forward onto the ischial-pubic ramus. The degree of this movement is determined by the individual person's build. The blocking effect of the ligament begins earlier the shorter it is. In the following section, the hip joint ligament will come up again, especially when discussing the chair seat.

MUSCLES

MUSCLES OF THE SEAT

Up to now we have primarily discussed the bones and sinewy tendons and mentioned the movement of the pelvis, the thigh and the spine. The muscles are also needed for movement. Let's turn now to examining those muscles that are especially important for riding. First, we need to know their location and function so we can understand how they act when riding and the sequence of movements that follows from their use.

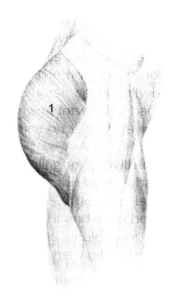

FIGURE 14.

1. gluteus maximus

Let's begin by describing the seat muscles. In Figure 14, we see the gluteus maximus, which covers the gluteus medius and minimus on the exterior of the ilium. In Figure 15, we see the gluteus maximus and the gluteus medius cut away, so that the gluteus minimus can be seen underneath. All three muscles extend from their originating position on the ilium to the upper end of the femur.

The effect of these three seat muscles on the thigh is a supporting one. Two of them are used to roll the thigh out; the smallest is the main muscle to roll the thigh in. When the large one is flexed, it hinders the pelvis from tipping forward.

MUSCLES OF THE THIGH
AND LOWER LEG

Of the large number of muscles in the area of the thigh we will discuss only those needed for riding in a special way. There are four muscles we will address more in depth. Do not be afraid of the Latin names, which we use for these muscles once. They will be called the riding muscles of the thigh, and we will use 'R' for the abbreviation of riding muscle and the numbers 1 through 4 for the individual muscles.

Next we will describe the location of the individual muscles. In Figure 16, we see on the front of the thigh the sartorius, R1. It originates from the front of the upper superior iliac spine of the pelvic girdle, runs along in a spiral fashion over the anterior side of the thigh and is attached underneath the knee joint on the interior side of the lower leg.

On the rear of the thigh (Figure 15), we see the semitendinosus, R2, and the semimembranosus, R3. Both originate from the rearside of the pelvic girdle, in fact on the ischial

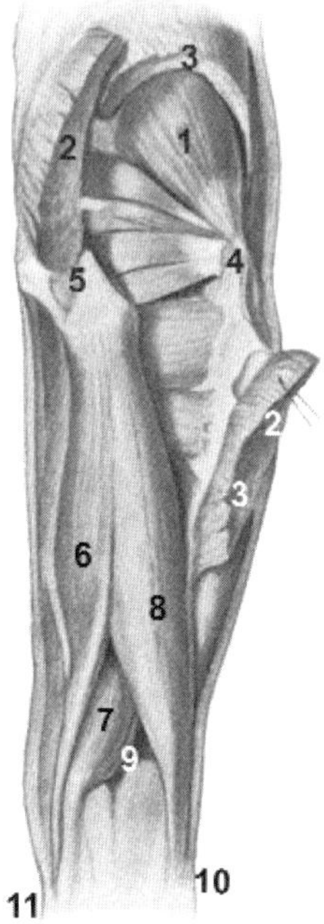

FIGURE 15. Rear of the Thigh

1. gluteus minimus; 2. gluteus maximus cut away; 3. gluteus medius cut away; 4. thigh bone; 5. ischial tuberosity; 6. semitendinosus; 7. semi-membranosus; 8. biceps; 9. knee joint 10. exterior of lower leg; 11. interior of lower leg

tuberosities, then run down along the inside of the thigh and are attached underneath the knee joint on the lower leg, close to where R1 is connected. The biceps, R4, originate just like R2 and R3 on the ischial tuberosities, go to the exterior of the lower leg and are attached close to the underside of the knee joint.

Now that we know where the muscles are, we will discuss the effects of their functions. All of them work to bend the lower leg; they draw the lower leg back and up against the thigh. More simply stated, you use them to bend your knee.

FIGURE 16. Front of the Thigh

1. sartorius; 2. adductors; 3. pubic crest; 4. anterior superior iliac spine; 5. knee joint

R1, R2 and R3 can also turn the lower leg at the knee joint to the inside. R4 can turn the thigh to the outside. The thigh can stay turned to the inside independently of R4. R2, R3, and R4, because of their origination on the ischial tuberosities, can pull the pelvis down. They are also helpful when tipping the pelvic girdle backward.

Because R1 originates on the front side of the upper superior iliac spine, it can pull the front part of the pelvic girdle downward. It can be helpful when tipping the pelvic girdle forward.

Now that we understand the functions of these muscles, let's summarize how the anatomical design of these relatively thin and long muscles make a variety of effects possible. They originate on the front or, as the case may be, rear side of the pelvic girdle. They bypass and—and this is essen-

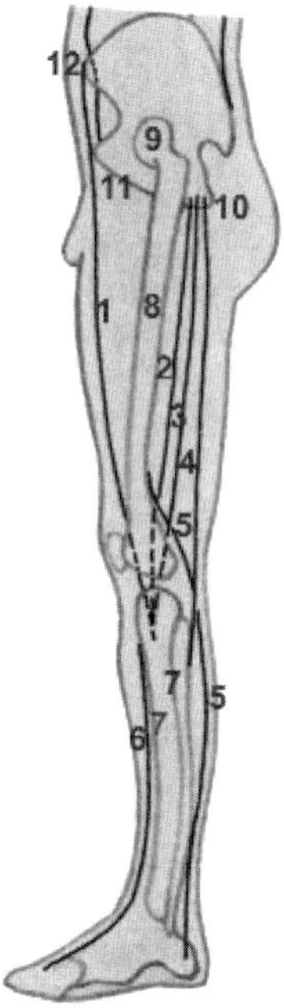

FIGURE 17. Schematic Representation of
the Thigh and Lower Leg Muscles

*1. R1; 2. R2; 3. R3; 4. R4; 5. calf
muscles; 6. extensor muscles of lower
leg; 7. tibia and fibula; 8. femur; 9. hip
joint; 10. ischial tuberosity; 11. ischial-
pubic ramus; 12. anterior superior iliac
spine*

tial—the hip joint, the femur and the knee joint. They are,
therefore, on both sides of the pelvic girdle: the front and the
back respectively. They act like pulleys in that they form a
direct connection from the pelvic girdle to the two lower legs
(Figure 17).

And what can the rider do with them? They give him
the possibility to move these three body parts together,
against each other, or independently of one another as needed. Because of this, he can carry out all combinations of
movements by the pelvis and lower leg that are required in
dressage. The rider can move the lower legs on one side or
both sides of the horse's body. He can turn them from the
knee joint without having to move the thigh. He can do this
with the legs no matter what position the pelvis, which is con-

stantly moving, happens to be in at the moment. Conversely, when these muscles are not being used to position the lower legs, he can use them to influence the position of the pelvis. This is because the muscles make it possible to pull the pelvis down, to support it while being tipped forward, backward or sideways, or when twisting; it is connected to all these movements. This we will now discuss.

The range of possible effects that this constellation of riding muscles allows are a gift from nature to the dressage rider. Everyone who pursues this sport will find it worthwhile to learn about them. When we deal with the demands of the riding instruction in the second part of this book, we will keep this in mind.

To conclude the discussion of the thigh musculature, let's look at Figure 16 once more. Here we see that inward

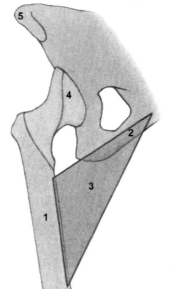

FIGURE 18.

1. femoral shaft; 2. ischial-pubic ramus; 3. adductors ("grippers"); 4. hip joint; 5. anterior superior iliac spine

from R1 on the inside of the thigh, there is a group of several strong muscles, the adductors. Their wide base of origin is on the lower ischial-pubic ramus. Where they are connected to the shaft of the thigh is just as wide (Figure 18). Compare this very massive, direct connection between the pelvis and the thigh to the thin riding muscles shown in Figure 17 and the direct connection between the pelvis and the lower legs.

In contrast to the spreading effect of the seat muscles, the function of the adductors is to exert a strong squeezing force. They are used to grip the thighs to the saddle. In addition, they have a strong stabilizing effect on the pelvis. They are able to not only hinder the motion of the pelvis, but to make it completely impossible.

FIGURE 19

1. extensor muscles of lower leg;
2. shin bone

We mention this group of muscles because it plays an important double role. The hunt seat rider would be lost without them. For the dressage rider, however, their use is the greatest sin of all dressage riding. With our index finger raised, we must warn emphatically against using them. We will also point out why they are so destructive for dressage riders. In the future, we will refer to them as the "grippers."

From what we have previously stated, we conclude that the thigh muscles R1 through R4 are intended to be used farther down to move the lower leg. In a similar fashion, the muscles of the lower leg exercise their function farther down on the foot and toes. On the front side of the lower leg (Figure 19) we have the extensor muscles that raise the foot and thereby indirectly lower the heel. They produce the foot position with the low heel that is required in riding.

On the back of the lower leg (Figure 20), we have the bending or calf musculature. It consists of several individual

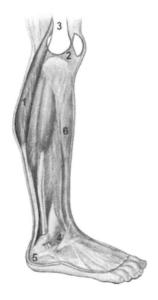

FIGURE 20.

1. calf muscle; 2. knee joint; 3. thigh bone; 4. ankle joint; 5. heel; 6. extensor muscles of lower leg

muscles. In our discussion here, we want to concentrate on just one: the calf muscle. It originates on the lower end of the thigh and bypasses the knee joint, the lower leg and the ankle joint, and is connected in the back on the spur of the heel bone. This arrangement is similar to the one we discussed for the riding muscles of the thigh. As a result, the calf muscle tenses, that is, becomes taut, as soon as one begins to bend the lower leg at the knee joint, provided the heel is deep and the ankle stays in the same position. When describing the use of the thigh, we will have to keep that in mind.

ABDOMINAL MUSCLES

The abdominal muscles of the anterior abdominal wall are the ones we will focus on here. They are in several layers, arranged in the same way on the right as on the left. We must pay special attention to three muscles. Here we see (Figure 21) the outer oblique abdominal muscle that originates on the outer side of the ribs, and runs forward and down at an angle. It connects to the iliac crest or merges with a ligament band in the abdomen's center.

At the next deepest layer (Figure 22), we see the inner oblique abdominal muscle. It originates on the underside of the iliac crest, and its fibers run up at an angle, unlike those of the outer oblique abdominal muscles. It is connected on the underside of the ribs and also merges into the same ligament band. The rectus abdominus (Figure 22) originates near the center of the lower edge of the ribcage, and runs straight down. It is connected to the front of the pubic bone on the pelvis.

The function of these muscles is mainly to comprise a section of the abdominal wall and to close the cavity. We must

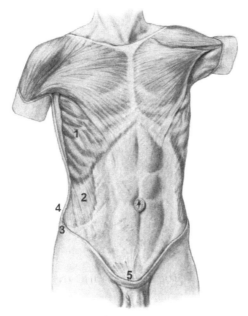

Figure 21.

*1. rib cage; 2. external oblique abdominal muscle; 3. anterior superior
iliac spine; 4. iliac crest; 5. pubic crest*

turn our attention to the fact that this muscle panel, arranged
according to a special pattern, which is stretched between the
lower edge of the rib cage and the foremost section of the
pelvic girdle, is especially important for the movements of
these two body parts. Here we want to be content with this
information. We will explain the function of the individual muscles while riding in the second part in the appropriate context.

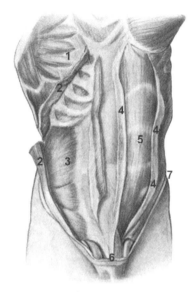

Figure 22.

1. rib cage; 2. external oblique abdominal muscle cut away; 3. internal oblique abdominal muscle; 4. external and internal oblique abdominal muscles cut away; 5. rectus abdominus; 6. pubic crest; 7. iliac crest

BACK MUSCLES

Finally, let's examine the back muscles. The surface layer of the broad back muscles (Figure 23) shows that the fibers run in various directions. Underneath the spine on both sides, a group of muscles stretches from the top to the bottom. They consist of various deep back muscles that are especially important for the movement and stabilization of the spine, the ribcage and the pelvis. As before, we can do without naming all of the individual muscles. In our discussion we will refer to them simply as the back muscles.

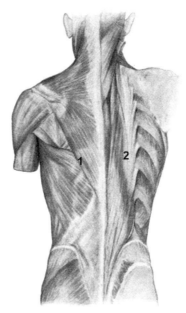

FIGURE 23.

1. surface muscles of the back; 2. surface muscles cut away revealing deep muscles of the back

Every medical student is glad when he has passed his preliminary medical examination. It means he has completed the theoretical portion of his studies, including the study of the anatomy. Subsequently he will be able put this knowledge into practical use in a clinical course of studies and as a doctor.

Similarly, let us now try to connect our anatomical knowledge with the demands of practical riding and riding instruction.

PART TWO

The Requirements of Riding from an Anatomical Perspective

THE SEAT: RESTING ON THREE POINTS OF SUPPORT?

In Müseler's *Riding Logic*, we read the following about the rider's seat: *The body rests vertically on the two seat bones and the crotch, which means on three supporting points*. Seat bones and crotch are very general terms which makes it difficult their exact location. Do we mean the two ischial tuberosities when we talk about the two seat bones? Is the ischial-pubic ramus what we would also call the crotch?

If we go back and reread pages 23–26, it becomes clear that three supporting points do not exist. Sitting on the two ischial tuberosities while at the same time sitting on a third bony point at the front of the pubic bone is anatomically impossible. We always sit on a narrow section of the ischial-pubic ramus, which we can rock more to the fore or to the rear by tipping the pelvis. We need this tipping motion of the pelvis as we will see shortly in our discussion about bracing the back, and we must be able to do it in varying degrees to the front and to the rear. This tipping motion would be impossible with a seat fixed on three bony points.

Let us point out that the rider's immobile pelvis is in constant motion as long as the horse is moving. All movements of the rider's pelvis happen at the base of the ischial-pubic ramus, which for the dressage rider is the equivalent of a ballet dancer's toes. The pedestrian can use the entire sole of the foot while the ballet dancer must position herself on the tips of the toes for her special exercises. A pleasure rider who only hacks out can use the entire breadth of his seat if he lets the horse carry him. In contrast, the dressage rider must lift his body onto the ischial-pubic ramus to perform correct dressage movements.

BRACING THE LOWER BACK

Bracing the lower back is considered to be essential in all riding theory. It is supposedly so important that every other aid that we want to give is dependent on it. According to Müseler, bracing the back is important when striking off, when halting and, *to sit in the saddle with varying degrees of contact, to stick to the saddle, to go with the motion of the horse.* No one doubts the necessity and importance of bracing the lower back. However, learning how to do it is difficult. To the question, "How do you do it?" you will not find a sufficient answer in any riding manual.

When we are asked to brace our back, we must assume that, anatomically, it is actually the sacrum that is meant. In this we agree with Müseler. In his side view illustrations of the spine and pelvis, he clearly shows the motion of the sacrum using arrows (Figure 24a). This corresponds to what we showed in Figures 9 and 10. In the illustration's caption, Müseler says, *When bracing the small of the back, the*

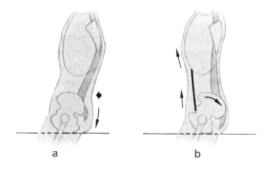

a   b

FIGURE 24. Bracing the Back

a. illustration according to Müseler; b. bracing the back by using the abdominal muscles with a stretched spine lower end of the spine (with the sacrum, which forms the connection between the spine and the pelvis) is pushed forward. Thereby the pelvis is pushed down and back, and lifted up in front.

Even here we agree because this corresponds to the tilting of the pelvis we explained on pages 24–26.

In reference to the question, "How do you do it?", we read in Müseler:

Using the small of the back in the first lessons is just as easy or just as difficult as it is later. One can brace the muscles of the small of the back to the same varying degrees as every other muscle, and accordingly give every aid with more or less bracing of the small of the back. One can brace the small of the back to hinder the seat from sliding backward, and one can also relax the small of the back. Therefore, it is not about doing different things.

Do we now know how it should be done? Hardly.

Theoretically, it should have become quite clear what should be done: use the muscles of the small of the back. Müseler can be read forward and backward, but you will not find either in his or anyone else's riding manual information that does more than outline what this extremely important musculature of the small of the back actually is.

In the anatomical portion of our discussion, we spoke of the seat, thigh, lower leg, abdomen and back muscles. We did not write about the musculature of the small of the back. This is not because we forgot about it. No, we could not write about it because it does not exist.

This may seem shocking, but from an anatomical perspective, it is fact that cannot be change, and one that we must recognize.

With this conclusion, the question still remains, With what can I brace the small of my back? If the sacral bracing muscles don't do the job, there must be other muscles involved. On page 19, we showed that the sacrum belongs to the self-contained pelvic girdle, and that we can only move it when we move the entire pelvis. Because we agree with Müseler that the pelvis tips backward when bracing the back, we have to look for the muscles that are responsible for this, and the result is that it is the abdominal muscles! To be more exact, it is the muscles that comprise the front part of the abdominal wall, which we have described on pages 41 and 42 (Figures 21 and 22).

It is, naturally, not so obvious that you would think of using the abdominal muscles in the front if you are told to brace the small of your back. It would occur even to a doctor only after a little more careful thought about the muscle functions and the sequence of movements.

An excellent rider and trainer, Müseler deserves all the more respect. He felt and portrayed the sequence of movements completely correctly because of his fine feeling for riding. He could not say, however, how and with what he managed to accomplish this pelvic motion due to a lack of more exact anatomical knowledge.

Let's adhere to the following: Bracing the small of the back is not caused by tensing, but rather by tilting. The sacrum is tipped to the rear such that the pelvic girdle, which includes the sacrum, is raised forward and up with the muscles of the front part of the abdominal wall (see pages 23 and 24, Figures 9, 10).

If we tense the abdominal muscles on both sides at the same time and to the same degree, we pull the front half of the pelvic girdle up, whereby the back half of the pelvic girdle tips backward around an axis that runs through both hip joints. This happens when riding a halt, for example.

If we tense just one side of the abdominal muscles, we cause a series of movements that consists mainly of a sideways tilting of the pelvic girdle, if the rectus abdominus predominates. The more the inner oblique abdominal muscle is used, the more the pelvic girdle tips to one side and twists. This is because the affected half of the pelvic girdle is not only tipped but, at the same time, pulled forward. Remember that the pelvic girdle is fixed and inflexible. To the same degree to which one half of the pelvic girdle is lifted to one side and turned forward, the other side must lower and turn backward. This happens when we ride curved lines and lateral movements. We will explain this in detail later on.

Let us remain with Müseler's description, which states that when the pelvis is tilted, the lower end of the spine is pushed forward. He points to this in Figure 24a by using an arrow that runs perpendicular to the lumbar spine. We have shown that the lumbar spine loses its forward curvature and approaches the vertical as in Figure 24b when the pelvis is tilted backward. This motion of the lumbar spine continues on to the thoracic spine, when we use the back muscles to stretch the thoracic spine, whereby its backward curvature decreases. In this way, we become more erect. "Sit taller," is the phrase riding instructors often use when they want us to perform this movement (Figure 24b).

The old riding instructors perceived the value of "sitting taller" based on their experience. In our view, its value lies in that the joint between the 5th lumbar vertebra and the sacrum becomes freer, and tilting the pelvis becomes easier. Our ribcage is lifted and becomes fixed in this position. Through this, our abdominal muscles can then work more effectively because they can be used entirely to lift the front half of the pelvic girdle. If the ribcage is not lifted, the abdominal muscles will pull the ribcage down instead of lifting the pelvic girdle up. Because the ribcage is relatively heavy, this happens quite easily. Then, the tilting of the pelvis when bracing the back is greatly weakened and could become completely impossible. The instruction to look straight ahead and not down is aimed at achieving the same result. The rider who looks down rounds his back and does not sit erect.

We do not want call the arrow wrong that goes from right to left at the parallel to the upper iliac crest in Müseler's illustration in Figure 24). When tipped, the pelvis can slide to the front to a greater or lesser degree depending on how much the back is braced. What is more important, however, is that the diagram does not show the lifting of the spine, nor the fact that it is primarily the front part of the pelvic girdle that is lifted by the abdominal muscles, which causes the back part of the pelvic girdle to be lowered. We think it necessary to point this out so that it is clear that the rider that must use his anterior abdominal muscles in order to brace his back. (Figure 24b).

The photos taken from Müseler's riding manual (Figures 25–27) clearly show the varying degrees of bracing the back.

FIGURE 25. RelaxedBback at Working Trot

FIGURE 26. Braced Back in the Transition to Medium Trot. The "Closed" Seat

FIGURE 27. Strongly Braced Back When Asking for Halt From MediumTtrot

USING THE LEG

Whenever we read about aids or influences on the horse, the back and the legs are mentioned in almost the same breath. Now that we have explained how to use the back, we will turn to the rider's legs.

From an anatomical standpoint we know that the thigh is turned inward by the smallest seat muscle, the gluteous minimus, and that its inner side should lie flat on the saddle. In this position, we are least tempted to use the grippers. Furthermore, this position of the thigh should result in the knee being as deep and as flat on the saddle as possible with the lower legs at or right behind the girth.

The task of the thigh is essentially to serve as a connector between the pelvis and the lower leg, in order to communicate to these two body parts the many possible aids of the riding muscles in the thigh, which is shown on pages 33–39. So that the thigh can fulfill this duty, it must be held as relaxed as possible in order to transmit the movement and coordinate the many pelvic and lower leg positions that change quickly. It cannot remain in the same position just described, that is, turned inward and with the inner side flat on the saddle. It must change this position when the motion of the pelvis demands so in order to return to the initial position. We will refer back to it in the appropriate context such as the twisted seat.

In the riding texts you will find differing opinions about the position of the lower leg and of the foot, which can be confusing for students seeking advice. The most common view is that the lower leg should fall at the girth, with the inner side lying flat on the horse, and the foot should be held parallel to the horse's body. "Turn your toes in" is a phrase instructors often use to bring their students in this position.

When we want to use the lower leg on the horse's body, we must bend it at the knee by using the riding muscles of the thigh. If we do so from the initial position just described in which the foot is parallel to the horse's body, the lower leg, which is also parallel to the horse's body, moves back and up, which causes it to become ineffective. Physically, it is possible to close the lower leg on the horse's body, especially its inner side, when our feet are positioned parallel to the horse's body. When we do this, the riding muscles of the thigh are not used but, instead, the grippers are. This immobilizes the pelvis, so that it can no longer go with the motion of the horse. In this position our legs cannot adjust to the motion of the horse in the correct manner because the knee joints cannot move sideways. In the trot, the legs are pushed off of the horse.

An optimal use of the lower legs can only be achieved when we turn them outward at the knee joint, with the foot at an angle of about 30 degrees. It is important to stress that this turning takes place in the knee joint. The thigh can remain independent in its position. From this position, the riding muscles of the lower leg can be applied in the easiest and most expeditious way by bending at the knee joint. In contrast to the position previously described with the feet parallel to the horse's body, the knee joint now allows for the horse's sideways movement against the rider's leg. The thigh and lower leg move against each other like a hinge, and the effect of pushing the thigh off the horse is cancelled out.

The riding texts demand that we keep our heels as deep as possible. This command is not only meant to keep the rider from continually annoying the horse with the spurs, but is also necessary and appropriate from an anatomical perspective. We wrote on page 39 that the extensor muscles on the front side of the lower leg lift the toes, which lowers the heel behind. We could leave it at that if some riding manuals and instructors did not claim that the deep heel is reached by stepping more heavily in the stirrups. A deep heel is achieved with both methods, but the results and accompanying occurrences of the different methods demand a closer look. This is mainly because of the different use of muscles.

It is critical to realize that when we step in the stirrups, we cannot use the riding muscles of the thigh to bend the lower leg at the knee. This is because during the process of stepping more heavily in the stirrups they are needed to stretch the thighs at the hip joint. The lower leg, however, and this is essential, cannot be drawn close to the horse in so doing, but rather moves away from the horse.

If, in contrast, we try to achieve a low heel by using the extensor muscles on the front side of the lower leg to lift the front part of the foot, unlike in the previous method, we can use the riding muscles of the thigh and simultaneously bend the leg at the knee. In so doing, the lower leg moves closer to the horse. Another advantage is that as soon as this bending begins, the calf muscle is flexed (page 40). Stress belongs on "begin," which means that we already can achieve a sufficient flexing of the calf with very little activity of the riding muscles, i.e., with little effort. With well-ridden and sensitive horses, this action is enough of an aid. If we need a stronger leg, we just have to use the riding muscles further by bending the knee more and bringing the lower leg closer to the horse. With this, we have a way to tune or control the amount of lower leg effect (Figure 28).

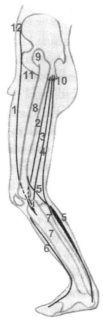

FIGURE 28. Using the Leg

1. sartorius; 2. semitendinosus; 3. semimembranosus; 4. biceps; 5. calf muscles; 6. extensor muscles of the lower leg; 7. tibia and fibula; 8. femur; 9. hip joint; 10. ischial tuberosity; 11. pubic ramus; 12. anterior superior iliac spine

The conclusion made with this anatomical perspective in mind is the following: Stepping in the stirrups and using the lower leg at the same time are mutually exclusive. These actions cannot be done at the same time because of the muscles involved. One might counter that certain riding exercises, such as picking up the canter, are easier when stepping deeper into the stirrup. Naturally, you can do this. Only you may not claim to have really used the correct leg aid to do so. The horse reacted to the shift in weight and not to the leg because the leg moved away from the horse. If you have trained your horse like this, you will also be able to ride it this way. We do not want to play judge and make any value judgments about whether this method or that one is more correct, but in the discussion of such questions,

undeniable anatomical principles can contribute to the explanation and objectivity.

From our point of view, one can summarize that a correct use of the lower leg is only possible from a position in
which the foot is at an angle of 30 degrees to the horse. From
here, the riding muscles of the thigh pull the lower leg, which
is bent at the knee, closer to the horse. The calf muscle flex-
es as soon as the bending starts, and the heel is lowered if
the front of the foot is raised with the extensor muscles of the
lower leg. The ankle is immobilized during the time the lower
leg is being used and released again after it is done being
used. (Figure 28).

Using the abdominal muscles makes an optimal bracing of the back possible. The riding muscles of the thigh allow
an optimal use of the lower leg. There is a collaborative muscle system from the pelvis to the toes. The back and the legs
can be used independently and individually as described in
the beginning of this section, and you can also use them in
combination of those muscle systems described. But we
want to hold off on that for the discussion of the halt.

The effect of the leg on the horse, forward and sideways driving, etc., has been extensively discussed in the riding texts. Now we would like to answer the question, "How do
you do it?" with reference to the use of the legs.

GOING WITH THE MOTION
OF THE HORSE

Before we turn to this topic, let's remember what we've
said about the regulating of the pelvic tilt by tipping the pelvis
forward or backward (pages 21– 24, Figures 9 and 10). This is
done only momentarily and indeed for a short space of time
as necessary, when the back is braced, for example.

In contrast, when going with the motion of the horse, our pelvis continually moves in a sideways direction as long as the horse moves. What happens during this process that is so important for the rider?

We must remember that our pelvic bone forms a fixed ring with the sacrum, so that the two halves of the pelvic girdle cannot be moved independently of one another. The rider usually is sitting on a horse that is moving, with the exception of the brief time spent at the halt. The horse's body alternates between lifting and lowering left and right in the walk and trot. If our pelvic girdle, which is closed, is supposed to adjust to this movement, and if possible to be brought into complete harmony with this motion, it must parallel the right and left lifting and lowering. It must lower to the same degree on the right as lift on the left and vice versa, whereby it falls into a sideways tipping motion.

The pelvic girdle is connected on the side to the two hip joints and at the top to the vertebra through the joint between the 5th lumbar vertebra and the sacrum. These sideways tilting movements can only take place if they are not hindered in the above-named joints, that is, when these joints are totally relaxed.

If we sit totally relaxed and with our legs hanging down loosely on a horse that is moving quietly, then our pelvis will passively adjust to the alternating lifting and lowering motion of the horse. This up and down motion of the pelvis will create a relaxed leg that is hanging down and automatically falls on the horse's body, on the side on which the horse's body and the affected half of the rider's pelvis lower. This downward motion of that half of the pelvis and the leg coming into contact with the horse's body happens exactly at the moment when the horse swings his hind leg forward on that same side. The deepest point of this downward motion of the pelvis is reached when the horse's forward swinging hind leg has just pushed off from the ground.

If the motion of the horse becomes fidgety or the horse starts to trot, we cannot keep this purely passive seat on the horse because we will lose our balance due to the jolting effect of the horse's back, which threatens to unseat us.

What should we do in order to stay in the saddle? If we go with Müseler in *Riding Logic*, we read, *The rider uses his legs and the muscles of the back to suck himself onto the saddle. The higher the horse bounces up and down and the livelier the tempo is, the more one has to brace the back., The bracing of both sides of the back is necessary to stay in the saddle.*

Let's take a close look at Müseler's advice to "suck" ourselves onto the saddle. The idea of sucking is known to everyone. On the first day of life before one can even think or use his sense organs, he can suck. Now this person skilled in sucking is grown and has become a rider who knows how to make distinctions. He can suck a bottle empty with a straw, but he also knows that he better not suck on it if he is drinking beer from it. Rather, he must let it run into his thirsty throat. As a rider he must use his legs to suck himself onto the saddle. This type of sucking is unfortunately not innate. The attempt to do so results in a natural defense reaction of the body, which latches onto the saddle with the thighs and/or lower legs. In so doing, the rider commits what we called on page 39 the greatest sin against dressage riding: the use of the grippers (Figure 18). His pelvis becomes rigid and can no longer follow the motion of the horse. Let us examine the riding muscles of the thigh and their ability to "suck." For this, we best read pages 33–39 once more. From this follows everything about the activity of these muscles, which among other things allows the pelvis and the lower legs to be pulled down onto the horse. These functions are important to our discussion.

If the horse is going in a very quiet and even trot and only bounces a little bit, the riding muscles of the thigh that pull downward when the knee is deep are enough to hold the pelvis, which is tilting right and left, in the saddle. The legs swing in a vertical position down through the knee and ankle. That is not purely passive anymore but rather, with the use of the riding muscles, the beginning of an active going with the motion of the horse (Figure 29). If the tempo and the jolting of the horse's back increases, the use of the riding muscles is no longer enough to keep the seat in the saddle. In addition, the riding muscles are no longer available if we need to use them to apply the lower legs. Therefore, to be as Müseler said, it must be the musculature of the lower back that creates the sucking effect.

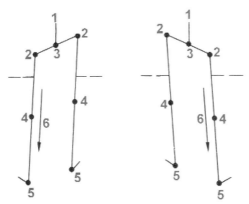

FIGURE 29. Actively Going with the Motion of the Horse with Help from the Riding Muscles of the Thigh on the Right and on the Left

1. spine; 2. hip joint; 3. joint between the fifth lumbar vertebra and the sacrum; 4. knee joint; 5. ankle joint; 6. direction of effect of riding muscles of thigh

From the section on bracing the back, we know that the musculature of the small of the back is actually musculature of the abdomen. We have also learned that we consistently tip the pelvis backward when we use the straight and oblique abdominal muscles simultaneously and consistently. This happens, for example, when we halt the horse. Now we do not, however, want to worry about the halt. We want to trot and thereby keep the left and right swinging pelvis in the saddle. For this, we must not use our abdominal muscles on both sides at the same time, but rather use them alternately, left and right, to pull the pelvic half that is lowering onto the saddle in this way each time. The livelier the tempo becomes, the more we must use the abdominal muscles (Figure 30). They have now taken over the task of the riding muscles of the thigh at a quieter tempo. Now it is the abdominal muscles that pull the pelvis down, allowing the thighs to swing straight down.

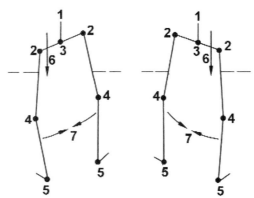

Figure 30: Going with the Horse with the Help of the Abdominal Muscles on the Right and Left

1. spine; 2. hip joint; 3. joint between fifth lumbar vertebra and sacrum 4. knee joint; 5. ankle joint; 6. direction of effect of riding muscles of thigh (with light contact)

And what do the riding muscles and the legs do now? They are now available to bend the leg at the knee and put the lower legs on the horse. We stress the expression "to put on" the horse because when the lower legs are relaxed in this position, they are in an especially favorable position from which to start. It is also a position of readiness. From this position, they can also pull the pelvis down to help the abdominal muscles keep the seat in the saddle. They can also leave this work to the abdominal muscles alone and put the lower legs on the horse as necessary instead.

That would have to happen, for example, if the rider wanted to increase the horse's tempo. He will not achieve this, however, by pressing his legs against the horse for a long time, but rather by using his legs briefly at the right moment. We have mentioned this right moment before when talking about the rider passively going with the horse's motion. It was the moment when the rider's relaxed leg comes into contact with the horse's body, which was when one half of the rider's pelvis lowers and the horse's hind leg on that side swings forward.

The rider pulls the respective half of the pelvis onto the saddle with the abdominal muscles alternating between the left and the right at the trot. He can support this with the riding muscles or he can use them to apply his lower legs. If he does the latter, he works on the active going with the motion at the same time as putting his legs on the horse. This causes the steps to lengthen and the tempo to increase. He is now doing as he is frequently instructed by the riding instructor, to "Drive!"

We want to emphasize that when going with the horse's motion, the reciprocity of the motion and the muscle activity are extremely important. Instead of talking about bracing the back on both sides, in this context one should speak of alternating the bracing in order to prevent the rider from thinking that when driving, he has to pull both halves of the pelvis into the saddle at the same time. Alternating motion of the horse and simultaneous motion of both pelvic halves cannot lead to harmony.

At shows, one often sees the anatomically incorrect seat being used at the trot. There are two versions of the incorrect seat. In the first version, the rider pushes the spine out to the back, leans back slightly and bounces roughly and with a rigid pelvis on the horse's back with each trot stride, with both sides of the pelvis bouncing at the same time. Understandably, the horse resents this, especially when the tempo is increased. The other version is when the rider tips his entire pelvis forward with every trot stride on both sides at the same time, and in this way increases the forward bending of the lumbar spine. The rider does not go with the horse's motion. Instead, the horse continually hits the rider's lumbar spine, which is swinging forward or backward. To the horse's back, the second method is always more pleasant than the first.

At any rate, failing to go with the horse's motion is a considerable burden for the horse's back and spine, but the rider's spine also suffers. The rider is not in the position to hold his spine up straight and stretched out because the jolting from below now feels unpleasant. He avoids the unpleasant jolting by pushing his spine rhythmically forward and backward.

Here we must ask you to turn back to page 15. There we described that the bending of the spine and the intervertebral disks are designed to alleviate the jolts that occur up the length of the spine. However, this construction does not suffice to fully cushion stronger jolts. For this, we must use additional measures, which we will now discuss.

If you try to jump with straight and locked knees from a low step, you will find it so unpleasant in the area of the spine that you will never try it again. Instead, you would try to cushion the effect of the jolt by bending the knee more or less according to the height of the step. Every gymnast does this when dismounting from his equipment.

Let us now return to the rider. If he would let his pelvis alternate between swinging left and right with the horse's motion by alternating the use of the abdominal and riding muscles with "through" joints as described above, he will achieve the same effect as the gymnast does when he bends his knees upon dismounting from the equipment. He will have neutralized the shock from below by swaying with the pelvis. This way he will be able to leave the spine stretched out, and to balance it quietly and without any unpleasant feelings in the joint between the 5th lumbar vertebra and the sacrum over the swaying pelvis, instead of pushing it rhythmically forward and back. We will delve into the function of the spine especially in the section on balance.

Some riders who trot in this incorrect way with a rigid pelvis are still able to keep their lumbar and thoracic spine halfway stretched, but only with great effort. They are no longer able to do this with the cervical spine, because the attempt would soon cause unpleasant headaches. Often they compensate for this with a more or less severe nodding of the head that corresponds to the rhythm of the trot.

Let us summarize: Going with the horse's motion means to harmonize the pelvis of the rider with that of the alternatively rising and lowering motion of the horse's body by alternating the activity of the abdominal muscles and the thighs. The back muscles stabilize the spine and, when necessary, activate a tilting forward of the pelvis.

In the canter, going with the horse is achieved by repeating the canter aids with every canter stride, which we will explain in a special chapter.

HALF HALTS AND FULL HALTS

The halt and half halt are also of special importance for and are dealt with in every riding manual. In Müseler, we read that the importance of the halt and half halt cannot be stressed enough for the rider's feel, seat and for the influence of the rider. A difference should be made between the full halt, which brings the horse to a halt, and the half halt. Half halts are used to shorten the tempo within a gait, in the transition to a lower gait, or to achieve increased collection with more elevated steps. If success is not immediate, the half halt should be repeated multiple times. How strongly the rider gives a half halt depends on the sensitivity of the horse. In a transition from extended trot to the halt, the half halts need be stronger and given more often than, for example, when transitioning from a medium trot to a collected trot.

The half halt is also used to prepare the horse for something new. Its purpose is to make the horse more attentive, and it also helps the rider to correct his position. The less experienced rider will first try to bring the horse to a halt or to a lower gait by pulling on the reins. He should learn to half halt as soon as possible.

To execute a half halt, the rider should activate his back, sit up tall, and use his legs. We have already discussed this way of carrying out the half halt from an anatomical perspective in the previous chapters, which were about the bracing of the back and the use of the legs (pages 21–26 and 35–40, Figures 9, 10). We can now refer back to it. First, let's discuss the full halt. In performing one, we tip both halves of the pelvis back equally by pulling up the front of the pelvis with the abdominal muscles on both sides. We have described this straightening and stretching of the spine forward and up in the section about the bracing of the back.

We want to emphasize that making the spine tall and straight means it has to go up and not backward. Simply leaning back, as one so often sees, is not the same thing as bracing the back and "growing taller" with the spine.

At the same time the rider braces his and grows "grows taller," he should hold the reins tighter and drive with his legs. You do this as we have described on page 56 by using the riding muscles of the thigh to bend the leg at the knee which puts the lower leg on the horse's body more or less forcefully, depending on the strength of the half halt. This causes the horse's legs to step under his body (Figure 31). To succeed with the half halt, the horse must be "through" enough so that the actions of the rider can be obeyed. A young horse that has not been trained enough will not be able

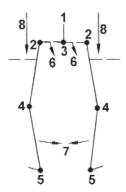

FIGURE 31. Full Halt

1. spine; 2. hip joint; 3. joint between fifth lumbar vertebra and sacrum; 4. knee joint; 5. ankle joint; 6. tipping the pelvis backward (abdominal muscles); 7. direction of effect of riding muscles of thigh; 8. direction of rein effect

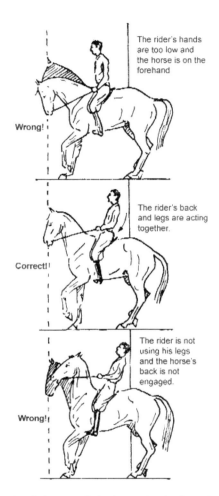

The rider's hands are too low and the horse is on the forehand

Wrong!

The rider's back and legs are acting together.

Correct!

The rider is not using his legs and the horse's back is not engaged.

Wrong!

FIGURE 32. Full Halt

to do this. But it's not our task to explain how to train a horse. You can read about this more comprehensively in the riding manuals. The sketches from Müseler (Figure 32) show clearly the effects of using correct and incorrect muscles when executing a full halt.

It should be pointed out here also that you should avoid using the gripper muscles when halting (Figure 18). The clinging that is associated with using them makes the pelvis rigid and it can no longer make the necessary tipping movement. When this happens, the rider makes the abdominal muscles compete with the gripper muscles, and in this case the grippers will win. When the thighs are gripping, you will not be able to tilt your pelvis and, therefore, a half halt is not possible.

Another possible hindrance to carrying out the full halt should also be mentioned. When the thighs are turned in too far, the hip joint ligament could prevent the pelvis from tipping backward (see page 27–31). A very slight turning of the thighs to the outside will be enough to relax the ligament so that the pelvis has the necessary freedom of movement.

Now we want to move on to the half halt and see what can be gathered from the riding manuals about its execution.

Müseler claims that the half halt should be performed in the same way as the full halt. This is perplexing and confusing for the riding student who is searching for an unambiguous and clear explanation. He also says to tip both halves of the pelvis backward simultaneously in the half halt, even though he mentions the possibility of just using one side in another context. For example, he says to use "one-sided bracing of the muscles in the small of the back to push the inner hip forward" when turning or when cantering.

Bürger summarizes the procedure of the half halt as sitting against the bit on the affected side.

Seeger tells the rider to hold the rein on the side that he wants to half halt more strongly and to put more weight on the corresponding hip.

Podhajsky recommends "the correct collaboration of leg, rein and the rider's back" to correctly apply the half halt.

In Steinbrecht, the prolonged holding of the reins is mentioned here and there, which should work together with the leg on the same side. The use of the back is not mentioned. Furthermore, Steinbrecht is of the opinion that the rider should realize and carry out the necessary aid with the hand and leg by feel. The rider who does not have this feel will never be able to acquire it because it cannot be taught. The momentary stepping of the horse's legs is too short for the teacher to address it in time, let alone for the student to be able to carry out a teacher's command in that brief moment.

We will not take refuge behind Steinbrecht's opinion about feel, but rather we will attempt to answer the question, "How do you do that?" from our perspective.

We cannot embrace Müseler's viewpoint that the full and half halt are to be done in the same way. To us, there is a clear difference. In the full halt, the entire pelvis is pulled up with the abdominal muscles on both sides at the same time. The back is thus tipped backward (bilateral bracing of the back). In contrast, in the half halt, the abdominal musculature on one side of the corresponding half of the pelvis is used to pull the pelvis forward and up (unilateral bracing of the back).

The spine is stretched at the same time by the back muscles. The lower leg of the affected side is placed on the

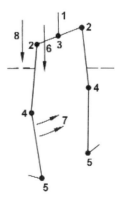

FIGURE 33. Half Halt Left

1. spine; 2. hip joint; 3. joint between fifth lumbar vertebra and sacrum; 4. knee joint; 5. ankle joint; 6. direction of effect of abdominal muscles; 7. direction of effect of riding muscles of thigh; 8. direction of rein effect

horse's body by the riding muscles of the thigh as needed. This unilateral use of the back and the legs results in increased pressure on the rein on that one side (Figure 33).

In general, the question, "How do you do that?" would now be answered for the half halt. But we would like to explain it more clearly and, indeed, in combination with the question "When do you do it?" It seems that the timing of the half halt is the difficulty that needs explanation.

From the riding manuals, we can gather that it is important to perform the half halt at the right moment. It should take place during the time when the horse's hind leg is stepping forward, and if it is to have a collecting effect, right at the end of the forward swinging movement, when the hind leg just leaves the ground. During these phases, the hind leg is in a bent position and cannot offer any resistance to the half halt. The horse can resist in the extended phase that follows.

If we have correctly interpreted the texts of the riding manuals, we must differentiate between: 1. a restraining half halt, which should take place during the phase when the simultaneous lowering of the rider's pelvic half and the forward swinging of the horse's hind leg occurs on the same side, and 2. a collecting half halt, which is to be carried out at the end of the phase of motion described under 1, when the horse's hind leg leaves the ground.

Let us think about how we can catch this favorable moment. Perhaps we will catch it most easily when we assume the rider is going with the horse's motion and we envision the execution of the movement. When the horse's right hind leg swings forward, the horse's right shoulder goes back. At this moment, the right half of the horse lowers along with the right half of the rider's pelvis. The deepest point of this downward motion on the right side is reached when the horse's right hind leg leaves the ground. Visually, the horse's right shoulder stops going back and begins to go forward again.

The rider pulls the pelvic half that is lowering towards the right onto the saddle. He does this with his right abdominal muscles during the phase when the horse's hind leg swings forward. The riding muscles of the right thigh can support the abdominal muscles by pulling the pelvis down. This would be going with the motion of the horse (Figure 30).

The riding muscles can also pull the lower legs onto the horse. When they do that with a giving rein, they induce the hind leg that is swinging forward to step forward more. This causes the strides to lengthen and accelerate, which is driving (Figure 34).

If, during the phase when the hind leg swings forward we use our back and our legs in the same way as before and do not give with the reins but instead take, we create a restraining aid, i.e. a half halt (Figure 33).

If we apply the half halt at the moment when the hind leg is setting down or extending forward to reach this point, it becomes collecting half halt that bends the hind legs.

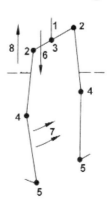

FIGURE 34. Driving

1. spine; 2. hip joint; 3. joint between fifth lumbar vertebra and sacrum; 4. knee joint; 5. ankle joint; 6. direction of effect of abdominal muscles; 7. direction of effect of riding muscles of thigh; 8. direction of rein effect

The very general instructions for executing the half halt in the riding manuals, such as "Sit against the bit" or "Take care that there is a correct combination of leg, rein and the back," should be explained, in our opinion. It can take a lifetime to learn to use the muscles correctly and at the right moment to execute the half halt. This can only be felt and, even then, it may never be perfect.

However, through knowing anatomy you can learn which muscles are to be used. The rider who can use the back with the abdominal muscles on both sides or on one side, and can apply the legs with the riding muscles of the thigh can also learn how to go with the horse's motion. As a consequence, he can also half halt.

With reference to the moment and the length of the half halt, which always has to be very short, initially you will have to risk a glance at the horse's shoulder to apply the half halt when the horse's shoulder on that side is moving back. This must be done without bending the head forward or the stretching of the spine will be impaired. Gradually you will succeed more and more in feeling the right moment. As you develop a feel for the right moment, you will increasingly do so without glancing down and only occasionally for reference. Hopefully, one day, you can do without it entirely.

The strength of the half halt can vary depending on how strongly you use the abdominal and riding muscles. It should be little if the half halt is intended to make the horse more attentive. On the other hand, we will use the muscles very strongly and repeatedly if need be if we want to half halt, for example, from the extended trot to the collected trot or to the walk.

BALANCE—GOING WITH THE MOTION OF THE HORSE

In the previous section, we spoke of the fact that the rider, in going with the motion of the horse, must balance over the swaying pelvis. We will explain this in more detail. The spine becomes an organ of movement in addition to its function as organ of support for the parts that surround it or are borne by it. It must provide for its own balance and that of the rider's in so doing.

Imagine there was a rigid connection between spine and sacrum, instead of a jointed one. Then the spine would be similar to a securely anchored mast on a sailboat (Figure 35). The mast goes along with every sway the boat makes, and the more the boat sways, the more the mast top tips. But because the swaying motion of the rider's pelvis, which is similar to the swaying of a boat, occurs much more quickly and rapidly, a spine that were rigidly connected to the pelvis could only go along with this quick tempo if the body mustered an enormous degree of muscle energy to set the spine in this motion. Besides, a pelvis of this design would not be able to handle the burden and would quickly become injured. All of this is avoided by the jointed connection of the lumbar spine to the sacrum, which gives the entire spine the ability to balance the motion at the lower end of the pelvis through a slight shift that does not require much exertion. Let us take an example to make this more clear.

FIGURE 35. The Movement of a Boat's Mast

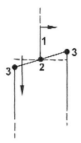

FIGURE 36. Action of the Spine when
Going with the Horse's Motion

1. spine; 2. joint between fifth lumbar
vertebra and sacrum; 3. hip joint

If a performer stands on a board placed on a barrel with legs spread out, he can only keep the board balanced, i.e., horizontal, if he leans with his body to the left when the board threatens to roll to the right, and he does the opposite with his body by leaning to the right when the board tips to the left due to being overweighted. Our spine does the same thing when riding. It compensates for the swaying motion of the pelvis when going with the horse's motion if we sit relaxed and "through." It does this through small, reciprocal weight shifts in order to remain vertical and in balance (Figure 36).

Let us make a few fundamental comments about a human's balance and then return to that of the rider. The balance of the entire human body is always unstable, i.e., continually shifting even while standing on steady, solid ground. Without a doubt we would fall over if we were to stand on a relatively small supporting surface, and our body did not continually make the appropriate muscle regulations and opposing regulations to prevent us from falling. In addition, it also uses weight shifts in order to keep the work of the muscles to a minimum in this continuous struggle for balance, similar to how we just described for the spine while riding.

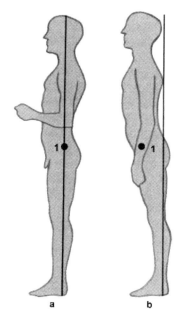

FIGURE 37. Position of Human
Body when Standing

a. normal posture
b. military posture
1. center of gravity located in pelvis

During the first two years of life a person learns with great effort first to sit, then come the first attempts to stand, and finally to stand with frequent tumbles and falls until one day he succeeds in standing and walking. He is only successful when the body has learned that when teetering to the right, to shift the weight to the left, and to use the appropriate muscles and counter actions. This process later occurs automatically so that we no longer notice it. Balance has been achieved in standing when the line of balance runs from the head through the body's center of gravity to its support point on the feet. Figure 37a shows the normal position. Notice that the center of gravity of the standing person lies in the pelvis at the third sacral vertebra.

This normal position can readily become an easy, unburdened position if, for example, we tip the pelvis backward until it is held only by the hip ligaments. In this way, the muscles are unburdened and energy is saved. One sees this position frequently in gymnasts who are on a team and have to wait until the equipment is available to them.

By contrast, in the tense military position, the body leans slightly forward. The taut seat muscles prevent it from falling over (Figure 37b).

Between these possible positions, there are a large number of variations. Any individual would generally not hold a specific position for longer than a minute. With every change in position, the center of gravity shifts and the use of the appropriate muscles to regain balance and to keep it change as well.

In riding the situation is different in so far as the rider's center of gravity is not down in the pelvis as when standing, but rather lies considerably higher in front of the 9th thoracic vertebra (Figure 38a).

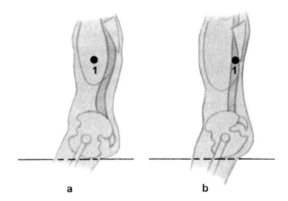

a   b

FIGURE 38. Rider's Center of Gravity

a. in relaxed position of spin, located in front of ninth dorsal vertebra;
b. in straightened spine, positioned at the ninth dorsal vertebra.

That point must be stressed, particularly in the illustrations of some riding manuals where the center of gravity of a standing person is used. The center of gravity of the rider and that of the horse should be one on top of the other, if possible, and should remain so in all riding situations. With the center of gravity at the ninth thoracic vertebra, a slight tilt of the body to one side or the other is enough to shift the rider's center of gravity over that of the horse. When performing riding exercises, it is even more necessary to hold the spine erect. We will remember this in our discussion of the spiral seat.

The vertical line, which runs from the rider's ear through the shoulder and the pelvis and goes to the heel, is often used as a criterion for the correct seat; it corresponds to the line of balance. It also runs through the horse's center of gravity.

We said earlier that the rider's center of gravity in the normal position of the spine lies in front of the ninth thoracic vertebra. The reason is that the thoracic spine in its normal position is curved toward the back. Depending on the degree of curve, the center of gravity lies closer or farther from the spine (Figure 38a). In addition, we spoke earlier of the fact that the spine must balance the forward and backward motion of the pelvis that occurs at its base while riding. A straight rod is more capable of balancing than a bent one. Therefore, we must straighten up and stretch, so that the thoracic spine's curve to the front and the lumbar spine's curve toward the back balance out and become as straight a rod as possible. It will then coincide with the line of balance. In this way, the center of gravity is not in front of the ninth thoracic vertebra anymore, but rather centered in it (Figure 38b). This creates ideal conditions for the balancing act of the spine, as well as for the creation and maintenance of the rider's balance.

The rider's body is substantially influenced by the forward motion of the horse. Forward is a fundamental requirement for the rider and the horse. When striking off and increasing the tempo, the body has the tendency to fall backward. In a vehicle that is starting off or accelerating, independent of whether it is a car, a bus or a train, every day we experience how our body is subjected to centrifugal forces and tends to fall backward. With the deep back muscles, the rider works against the centrifugal force and uses them to make sure that the spine, and with it the upper body, does not fall backward. When riding, we have the additional challenge of going with the horse's motion added to the spine's balancing act of sideways motion over the swaying pelvis, that is, going forward and backward. The balancing of the spine in this way is what we will call going with the motion of the horse.

In Müseler's riding manual, no clear difference between going "in" the motion and going "with" the motion of the horse is made. We think it necessary to clearly differentiate between these concepts, but for reasons other than that of semantics. From an anatomical perspective, the resulting series of movement and the conclusions that can be drawn from it can be better described, better defined in relation to each other, and made more understandable. In practice, both things overlap. It is not a question of either going in or going with the motion, but rather one of going in *and* going with.

In summary, it should be pointed out that the stretching of the spine is absolutely necessary and required for dressage riding. It must, therefore, be required of the rider. Stretching his spine will give the rider great advantages:

1. The joint between the fifth lumbar vertebra and the sacrum becomes looser. As a result, the pelvic motion becomes easier.

2. The abdominal muscles' ability to function increases when the spine is stretched, which raises the front of the rib cage.

3. The rider's center of gravity shifts to the ninth thoracic vertebra, which improves the balance of the spine and the balance of the rider.

Stretching the spine also has a disadvantage. It corrects the physiological curvatures described on page 15, which are there to protect the spine from jarring down its length. The rider can and must accept this disadvantage, because he can compensate for it in that he learns as quickly as possible to go in the motion of the horse (see pages 58–66). With that, he can prevent his spine from becoming injured or from taking refuge in evasive maneuvers, which we described in what we consider to be an incorrect seat at the trot.

SUPPLENESS AND GRIPPING

Suppleness, sometimes referred to as "looseness," is one of the essential requirements in all riding manuals. The bracing of the back, going with the motion of the horse, and the associated motion of the pelvis are only possible when there is nothing that impedes free movement. There are many ways in which free movement can be impeded. One of the gravest is when the rider gripping with the thighs, i.e., using the grippers (see page 38–39). There we have shown that the use of these muscles is a fundamental error in dressage riding. There is no rider who has not made this error when first beginning to ride, and there will certainly be more than a few who never entirely stop. There are several reasons for this.

The pressure of the saddle and the jarring of the horse on the muscles and the tendons on the inner side of the thigh cause these muscles to reflexively contract. Furthermore, we showed that the burden of the body when riding rests on the ischial-pubic ramus. Besides the breeches and undergarments, between the ischial-ramus and the saddle there are only the skin and a relatively thin layer of tissue under the skin and muscles of the perineum, i.e., the section between the anus and the genitalia. A special seat cushion is, unfortunately, not built in. In the beginning, it is easy to have pressure on the outside of the skin, and internally on the periosteum of the ischial-pubic ramus. This is unpleasant and causes pain. As a result, there is a reflexive defense mechanism of the body, which is anxious to keep the tender parts away from the saddle by tightening the grippers.

Another reason for gripping is that the rider has not yet learned to go with the horse's motion. He will at first be anxious to work against the centrifugal force, which he is subjected to especially when the tempo increases, by gripping with the thighs. He will also use the reins for support.

The rider accustoms himself to this if he is not educated and schooled properly. The already strong muscle group of the grippers becomes even stronger due to constant work. Eventually a bulge can develop, which no longer allows the rider to lay his thigh with the inner side flat on the saddle. Through effusions of blood, it can also harden. There have even been reports of ossification. Such extreme cases hopefully are rare because they are difficult to reverse, if at all.

Gripping is often caused when the horse is restless and bucks, for example. By tightly gripping with his thighs, the rider tries to survive the emergency situation that the bucking horse brings him into. He does not notice that he is doing something inexpedient. When gripping with the knees, he is thrown higher out of the saddle with every buck. After the third or fourth buck at most he will find nothing more to grip! If he does not hold onto the mane or is not spared by the horse quieting down, he will land in the sand. His riding instructor has probably yelled at him, "Sit in the saddle" or "Sit down behind," which means to use the abdominal muscles and riding muscles of the thigh, so that the seat stays in the saddle and the lower legs can be effective. In this way, the pelvis remains loose and can adapt to the motion. The rider survives the emergency situation with less effort because he uses the correct muscles. If supple and relaxed, he can apply himself to further dressage tasks.

Suppleness does not mean the opposite of gripping: hanging on the horse with floppy muscles. Suppleness means and comes about when the correct muscles are used at the right moment for the right amount of time for a particular situation in riding.

In summary, we can gather from what was said in this section that gripping is caused by the rider's body protecting itself from pain in the seat or from damaging consequences of centrifugal force, which threatens to bring him out of balance.

In that regard, gripping is a natural and purposeful reaction of the body which it does to protect us. Basically, we have to be thankful that our body is able to take such defensive measures automatically and puts them into action very quickly for our welfare. In dressage, however, this beneficial and well-meant course of action of our body is a hindrance. By using the grippers, our pelvis is made inflexible, which makes going in the motion of the horse no longer possible.

Through this we come into the peculiar situation in which the innate, well-meant defensive measures of our body may not be used to provide for the requirements of dressage. We have the impression that one of the essential reasons why dressage is so difficult for riders and instructors is hidden in this. We will have to explain this further but will postpone this discussion until we reach Part Four on teaching and learning.

THE CHAIR SEAT AND THE HOLLOW BACK

Another variation on the rider's reaction to unpleasant sensations in the seat area, which develops very easily in the beginning rider and then remains for a longer or shorter amount of time, is the so-called "chair seat." While before the reaction of the rider was gripping, in the chair seat his reaction is the extreme shifting of his seat to the back. The inclination toward comfort plays a role here, of course. It is more comfortable to sit to the back on the two pin bones, to pull the thighs up so that the lower legs are no longer at the girth but in front of it. This seat resembles that of sitting in a chair.

It is not difficult for the rider to let the horse carry him around using this seat. He cannot, however, ride dressage like this. In the riding arena, the instructor will tell him to bring his legs back so they lie at the girth. The result of this command is that after a few steps, the legs slip forward again. The instructor repeats his command several times over the course of the hour. The rider continually struggles with his hip ligament.

On pages 29–31 (Figures 13a–13c), we wrote about the position of the pelvis and the behavior of the hip ligament in this pelvic position. It is advisable to read that once again.

As long as the rider sits only on the pin bones with his pelvis tilted extremely backward, the hip ligament will not allow him to let his legs hang either at or right behind the girth. He must tip his pelvis more forward to roll the foundation of the seat from the pin bones more to the front onto the ischial-pubic ramus, even if it is uncomfortable in the beginning. He will have to continually try until the skin and the bones have become accustomed to it. When he has succeeded in this, he has acquired the advantage of the legs remaining at the correct place on their own. The pelvis now is also flexible instead of being fixed in its extremely backward tilted position.

The muscles that tip the pelvis forward are the back muscles, which can be supported by the anterior riding muscle R1. In order to let the back muscles become effective, the rider will have to be told again to sit up tall. Remember, he should also do that when bracing the back. But while he has to flex the abdominal muscles to tip the pelvis backward, the abdominal muscles are not used to straighten up because now they are needed to tip the pelvis forward. He also must not tense the gluteus maximus because this would block the tipping of the pelvis to the front. Straightening up with a relaxed seat would alone suffice to tilt the pelvis forward to the small degree required, which is necessary to relax the hip ligament.

It does not take as long to play this out as it does for us to describe it. The straightening up and the tilting of the pelvis, which is a small action, take only a matter of seconds. No instructor can tell the rider how many degrees he must tip his pelvis forward. Success is achieved when the pelvis assumes a position from which it can adjust the horse's motion and from which the legs remain lying at the correct position on their own. Soon the rider will also notice that if he

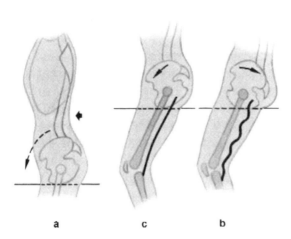

a   c   b

FIGURE 39. The Hollow Back

a. depiction according to Müseler
b. pelvis tipped forward; riding muscles of thigh flexed
c. pelvis tipped backward; riding muscles of thigh relaxed

is in danger of falling back into the chair seat, he can correct himself by straightening up.

At this point, it seems advisable to go into the illustration in Müseler, which has the caption, "hollow back" (Figure 39a). In the textual explanation, it is merely said that through this arises the opposing effect of bracing the back because the pelvis is tipped forward.

For the rider who reads this arises the impression that, first of all, tipping the pelvis forward is wrong and therefore should not be done. Secondly, tipping the pelvis forward is the reason for the "hollow back."

Before we give our opinion on both, it must be first pointed out that a few things are getting messed up in regard to terminology. The sacrum is hollow at the front (Figure 1). It is a rigid bone on whose hollow form nothing can be changed, no matter what position it is in. What Müseler means by "hollow back"—and this is apparent from his sketch and is shown in a similar way in other riding manuals—is a lumbar spine that is bent too far forward (Figure 39a).

And now we want to comment on the two points mentioned above.

1. Tipping the pelvis forward is not wrong. In certain positions of the pelvis such as in correcting the chair seat, is absolutely necessary. In this situation and in others similar, it must be done in order to allow the pelvis to adjust to the motion of the horse. Please remember what we said about the pelvic tilt and about the role of the hip joint ligament. The position of our pelvis is unstable over the horse's back, which is to a large degree continually in motion. It can only adjust to this motion when the pelvis can be tipped and turned to the same degree to the back, front and to the side.

2. The "hollow back," when the lumbar spine is bent too far forward, is not caused by tilting the pelvis forward. The riding muscles of the thigh R2–R4 see to that. When we bring the pelvis to the most extreme tipped back position, the riding muscles of the thigh relax so much that they become loose (Figure 39b). When we tip the pelvis forward from this backward tipped position, these muscles, which go like drawstrings from the pin bones to the lower legs, tense up more and more (Figure 39c). In this way they prevent the pelvis from tipping too far forward. Because of this, the pelvis can never tilt forward so much that it causes an exaggerated bending of the lumbar spine towards the front. No, the cause of the "hollow back" lies in the spine itself, which the rider either cannot or will not hold up straight and stretched.

When the cause for not sitting up straight is too little willpower, ignorance or weakness of the musculature, it can be corrected. If it is, however, a pathological change in the spine, which is not only in the area of the lumbar spine but also can be in the thoracic spine, it must be checked out and then determined if one may ride at all.

THE USE OF THE SEAT MUSCLES

An additional danger that can impede the pelvis in its mobility lies in the use of the seat muscles. We have already hinted at that. Because they lie next to the sacrum, it is easy to confuse them with the "muscles of the small of the back," and continually try to use them to brace the back. After what we wrote on pages 32–33 about these muscles, this attempt must fail. This failure has resulted in some riding manuals saying never to use them. However, this negative blanket judgment is also wrong. We must use these muscles because, without their use, we could not spread the thighs and turn them inward to bring them flat onto the saddle. We simply must use them for these functions for which they are made. To brace the back, we must use the abdominal muscles. The seat muscles are inappropriate for that. The incorrect use of especially the gluteus maximus will hinder us in tipping our pelvis forward. This is still a small sin compared to that of using the grippers.

THE SPIRAL SEAT

In our previous discussions, we assumed that the horse is moving straight ahead. In the arena, though, we also ride on curved lines: in the corner, on a circle, in a volte. We also ride lateral movements. What do our riding manuals say about this?

Wätjen writes, "Furthermore, the rider must see to it that he does not twist his upper body in the lateral movements, but rather remains sitting vertically and does not hang to one side, and does not drop a hip, but rather keeps sitting up straight and goes with and in the motion of the horse, continually with one shoulder parallel to the horse's shoulder."

Müseler requires that the rider's hips be parallel to the horse's hips, and the rider's shoulders also be parallel to those of the horse.

Steinbrecht's comments on this are quite detailed: "The rider must support the work of the hand and leg with his seat, in that he takes up the correct position artificially for the time being, which the correctly bent horse shows him by itself. I mean the seat, by which placing the inner hip puts the outer leg back more, the inner forward, and when riding on curved lines, the inner seat bone is weighted more. The artificial position of his hips should not be transferred to his shoulders, however, because a forward inner shoulder places the outer one back. While on a curved line, where the outer shoulder of the horse describes a larger arc and is well in front, the rider should also put his shoulders forward. Our hips and shoulders must work in opposite directions, which is a task that is only solved by a few riders. This is because it seems for most riders easier and more natural to hold both evenly positioned in the same direction. This rider's seat, to which I will return to in future discussions of bending, and which we will call 'the spiral seat' for simplicity's sake, is correct (this is also sometimes called the 'turning seat'). It is elicited through the position of the horse when the rider no longer has to maintain it by artificial means such as squeezing thighs and pushing the hip and shoulder forward, but goes passively in the motion, in other words, sits in complete harmony with the horse."

In all three quotes, it becomes clear that when riding on curved lines, the rider's hips should be positioned parallel to those of the horse and the shoulders parallel to those of the horse. Our question "How do you do that?" arises again.

Which dressage rider has not continually tried hard to understand that? He hears the instructor's command, "Push your inner hip forward!" As soon as he does that, he hears, "Why are you letting your outer shoulder hang back? Push your outer shoulder forward!" So he puts his shoulder forward, and his inner hip goes back. Damned uncomfortable, this horrible twisting! Steinbrecht seems to be right in his conviction that only a few can accomplish this task. We will have to concern ourselves with the pushing forward of the hips and shoulders. Push them forward how and with what? We have noticed that Steinbrecht at another point says to "position" forward rather than "push" forward, almost as though he himself was not quite sure that the process of positioning a hip forward is also one of pushing forward.

Let us proceed from the fact that a rigidly closed pelvic girdle evenly alternates from left to right in the motion of the horse when we ride on straight lines. The abdominal muscles and the riding muscles in the thigh provide for this. In the section about going in the motion of the horse, we described this. Now we are riding on a circle, but going with the motion of the horse may not stop because it is a curved line. Our bodies must adjust to the new situation. Let us assume, in order to eliminate misunderstandings, that we are going to the left. Because the horse is bent to the inside, the inner hip of the rider, in this case the left hip, should be pushed forward. The demand to push forward contains the risk that we will use the gluteus maximus, blocking the inner pelvic half and the hip joint. It is not possible to go with the motion of the horse like this. Instead of pushing, we try to pull, for which we again use the abdominal muscles unilaterally.

In going with the motion of the horse on a straight line, the pelvis, which is straight, goes up and down. The downward motion is supported by the abdominal muscles, principally by the straight abdominal muscle muscles on the affected side. Now on a curved line, the inner half of the pelvis is pulled forward, which also comprises the inner hip. In addition, the left side of the abdominal muscles must be used more in the direction of forward than backward. The inner oblique abdominal muscle on the left side is more strongly activated and pulls the left half of the pelvis forward. It can only do that if, in full relaxation, the hip joint and the joint under the fifth lumbar spine allow the other half of the pelvis to go backward to the same degree.

In this new position, the pelvis must swing as long as you are riding on a curved line, going in the motion of the horse to the right and left. The rectus abdominus and the inner oblique abdominal muscle on one side work together in order to swing with the motion. They go in harmony with the new pelvic position on the left hand from front left at an angle to back right. Going to the right it is the opposite. This type of motion can best be described as a turning-tilting motion.

The legs, which hang on the outside of the pelvis, play a part in the turning of the pelvis. The left leg and its half of the pelvis is forward and the right leg with its half of the pelvis goes back, where it lies as desired right behind the girth.

While we could hold both thighs turned inward while riding straight ahead, their position now has changed. When pulled forward, the inner half of the pelvis and its hip turns a little to the outside. The outer thigh with its hip, turned backward, turns a little to the inside. Those are small turning moments that appear outwardly only a little or not at all.

If we do not turn the thighs in the way described, then the abdominal muscles cannot carry out the desired pelvic motion. With rigid thighs, the pelvis can only be moved around a single axis, which goes at an angle through the pelvis and the two hip joints. If the direction of the axis must be changed, the thighs must turn with it in the described way. That they may not be gripping while doing this is an obvious prerequisite for the execution of this turning. At the same time, they must also remain connection links to the lower legs, which must remain relaxed and ready for use independent of this entire turning process, so that they can be used as necessary via the riding muscles of the thighs.

With that we have solved the first half of this difficult task. We have met the demands of the riding instructor to bring the inner hip forward. In so doing, we go with the motion of the horse, and our hips move parallel to those of the horse. They do not stay still, but rather move parallel to those of the horse.

Now comes the second part of the task. The outer shoulder should also be forward. Naturally we can push it forward with the muscles of the shoulder and the back, but we already tried that. The result is that the inner hip slips back again and the struggle between hip and shoulder begins again.

If it were helpful to pull the inner hip forward, why should it not be helpful to pull the outside shoulder forward? Perhaps some insight and the thought emerge, "They want us to move the shoulder with the abdominal muscles as well."

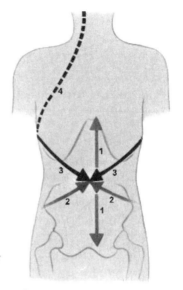

FIGURE 40. Spiraling Muscle Paths

*1. rectus abdominus; 2. internal
oblique abdominal; 3. external
oblique abdominal; 4. muscles of the
back and neck*

This inkling is not wrong. This is our intention and we
will explain and justify it.

Let us look at Figure 40. The path of the muscle fibers
of the abdominal muscles is shown here schematically (compare to Figures 21 and 22). The fibers of the rectus abdominus appear as a vertical line in Figure 40. The fibers of the
internal oblique are gray; the external oblique abdominal muscles are black. It is noteworthy that the gray fibers, starting
from the lower left, continue their direction at an angle to the
top right, parallel to the black. In the continuation of this direction, diagonally up around the rib cage over the back to the
neck, more muscles with the same fiber direction, which are
depicted by dashes, join in. We have, in this way, a spiraling
pattern of muscles going in the same direction, which extends
from the pelvis' lower left, diagonally over the belly to the

ribcage's upper right on around to the back and neck. On the other side, it goes in the opposite direction respectively.

Let's examine the manner of this spiraling effect. The important thing is that it arises from individual, generally independent muscles, which can work together in the direction of the spiraling because all the fibers run in the same direction. They all run in a row as if they were one muscle. In anatomy theory, this is called kinematic chains. On the other hand, these muscles do not have to have effect only in the direction of the spira, as if they were a track that allowed no other movement. They can be effective individually or as a group. Active and passive components of the motion can work together as necessary. The body will always be able to deal with any situation.

And now we return to the spiral seat. We got to where the left inner oblique abdominal muscle pulled the left hip forward. Our desire to pull the right shoulder forward meets the next muscle of the spiral, which is now the right outer oblique abdominal muscle. When it is activated, the right half of the rib cage is pulled forward. The right shoulder, which takes part in the motion, is attached to it and also moves forward. When riding a circle, the degree of turning the rib cage achieved by the outer oblique abdominal muscle is enough. If more turning is required, such as when the arc to be ridden becomes smaller or when riding lateral movements, the turning can be continued with the help of the back and neck muscles, which turn farther in on the spiral.

Now we come to the point where the left hip and the right shoulder have moved forward in an opposing motion. And now our hips move not only parallel to the horse's hips, but also our shoulders are parallel to those of the horse. We have achieved what Steinbrecht calls the "bent seat," a term that is derived from the bent position of the horse. We would prefer "spiral seat" in order to base it on the turning motion of the horse. The name hints at what is required. The seat should turn, not bend.

When the seat bends, the spiraling cannot be effective, and the rider uses incorrect muscles. In the use of the term "bracing the back" we have already seen how easily one terminology can lead you down the wrong path regarding which muscles to use. The bending of the rider would also increase the risk that the spine no longer remains vertical. Even with comparatively little bending, the center of gravity at the ninth thoracic vertebra would shift so far out that it is no longer over the horse's center of gravity.

The spine must remain vertical and stretched throughout this process. The counter rotation of the pelvis and the rib cage with the shoulder is not around the axis of the spine. The spine is actually involved in this spiraling process. The construction of this multi-jointed rod allows its lower and upper ends to turn in opposite directions at the same time. Now twisting in opposite directions, the spine must be kept vertical and balanced over the swaying pelvis.

In the spiral seat, this muscle spiraling allows us to fulfill all of the individual demands we quoted at the beginning of this chapter from the riding manuals. The spiral seat harmoniously solves what we cannot achieve by using uncoordinated muscles to push sometimes up and sometimes down, because to carry out the series of movements we use muscles that bring about perfect cooperation.

We want to summarize once again the importance of the abdominal muscles. With them we can:

1. Tip the entire pelvis back (bilateral bracing of the back). The pelvis tips around a horizontal axis that runs through the pelvis and the hips.

2. Pull the pelvis forward on one side (beginning of the spiral seat). The pelvis turns around a vertical axis that runs through the middle of the pelvis.

3. Tilt the pelvis sideways on one side, sideways and backward respectively (going in the motion of the horse, unilateral bracing of the back).

4. Pull one-half of the rib cage forward.

In Figure 17, we saw the pelvis connected by the cord-like riding muscles of the thigh down to the lower legs. Figure 41 shows us how the pelvis hangs between the abdominal and back muscles. On page 58, we spoke of the coordinating muscle systems from the pelvis to the tips of the toes. Now we have learned about muscle systems that work just as well from the pelvis to the head. These muscle groups above and below the pelvis can function together in an ideal way. The pelvis can be tipped forward, sideways, backward. And in connection with or independently of this tipping, it can also be turned. The use of the lower legs can be combined with these movements as needed or be carried out independently of them.

In describing the riding muscles of the thigh, we spoke of the gift of nature to the dressage rider. Now we should definitely be convinced that nature programmed us in the most generous way to ride dressage. It only depends on recognizing and using the given possibilities.

Let's read once again the conclusion of the Steinbrecht quote at the beginning of this chapter where he writes that riders who have mastered the spiral seat go passively in the motion. This, of course, he cannot do. No person can ride half pass in the spiral seat without actively using his muscles.

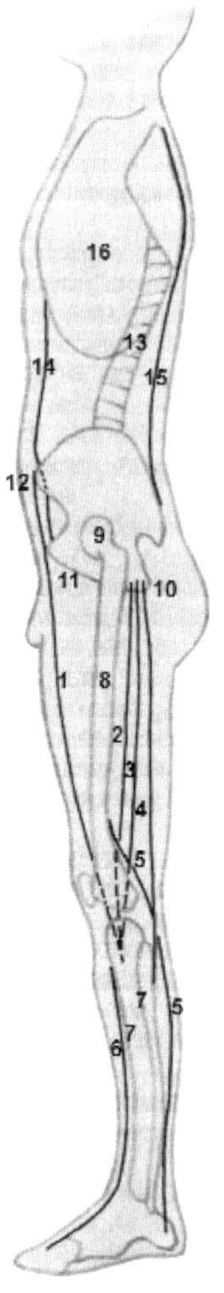

FIGURE 41. Schematic Representation of the Muscle Systems Above and Below the Pelvis

1. sartorius; 2. semitendinosus; 3. semimembranosus; 4. biceps; 5. calf muscles; 6. stretching muscles of lower leg; 7. tibia and fibula 8. thigh bone; 9. hip joint; 10. ischial tuberosity; 11. ischial-pubic ramus; 12. anterior superior iliac spine; 13. spine; 14. abdominal muscles; 15. back muscles;

Because of Steinbrecht's unusual riding talent and experience, he was in the position to use the correct muscles without knowing about them. The muscle exertion was so miniscule for him that he had the feeling that he was not using any muscles. This is the way the greats of the sport make dressage seem even today, as the two photographs taken from Müseler (Figures 42 and 43) clearly show how the spiral seat is done especially well.

FIGURE 42. Spiral Seat:
Left Lead Canter Through
a Corner

FIGURE 43. Spiral Seat:
Left Lead Canter on a
Straight Line

RIDING THROUGH THE CORNER

In the previous section, we determined that we use the spiral seat on the curved lines of lateral movements. We also use it when cantering. In general, one can say that we always need it when the horse has to be positioned to the right or to the left. Let us look at a couple of practical lessons connected to this.

When riding through the corner, the rider leans into the curve like a bicycle rider. Now note that a bicycle is called a "wire donkey" in German vernacular. No one has ever named it a "wire horse." Thus, you may ride like a bike rider on a donkey, but never on a horse. Nothing is meant by this either against bike riders or donkey riders. We hope that after reading the previous chapters it is clear why you must not lean into the curve. The center of gravity would no longer be over the horse, the rider's inner hip and outer shoulder could no longer turn in the correct position, and his legs would no longer be in the right place.

The horse responds to the bike-rider seat when ridden through the corner by not going as he is supposed to, which causes the instructor to admonish, "Your outer leg is not there."

The precept is that the horse should go through the corner bent but straight, i.e., the lateral bend of the horse's spine should correspond to the curve of the arc being followed. His hind legs should follow exactly in the footsteps of his forelegs. In the beginning of training, this is as uncomfortable for the horse as the spiral seat is for the beginning rider. Because leaning into the curve makes life easier for the horse, he does the same thing as the bicycle-riding rider by not completing the lateral bend, which causes his hind end to fall out.

Why should there not be equality between the rider and the horse? Both trundle cozily through the corner in chummy and comfortable companionship. The instructor does not like this, of course, and reminds the rider again about his outside leg (which the rider should take heed of immediately).

It will be different in the next corner, the rider vows. So, before the corner he gives a half halt, then uses the spiral seat. What we needed so much time for to describe verbally takes place almost instantly: the inner half of the pelvis is pulled forward with the inner oblique abdominal muscles, and the inside leg is at the girth; the outer half of the pelvis goes back to the same degree along with the outside leg; the outer shoulder is pulled forward with the outer oblique abdominal muscles. The pelvis must sway in a relaxed manner in the motion of the horse, even in this twisted position. Now that the rider is especially attentive, he can even count inwardly: one, two, three, four times his pelvis sways in the twisted position. The rider can now go through the corner with his horse bent properly. He can transition back to the normal seat on the straight line. The instructor smiles, satisfied.

In the case just described, riding through first the corner did not succeed because of reasons of comfort. It also cannot succeed if the abdominal muscles are unable to perform the spiraling. When we move the pelvis while standing, the well-lubricated hip joints offer no special resistance. Move the pelvis in the saddle and the movement will also roll through the loose hip joints, but now the hip joints carry more weight. The entire body weight rests on the ischial-pubic ramus (Figure 11). In the spiral seat, the inner oblique abdominal muscle must pull the entire body weight onto the inner ischial ramus. The surrounding soft parts increase resistance and, therefore, the work. The thighs should lay loosely on the saddle, but when are they ever so loose that they do not offer any resistance? If the abdominal muscle is too weak, it cannot complete its task. It cannot do so in the same way that too weak upper arms biceps make it impossible for a gymnast to perform a pull-up. As school children, we tended to name these poor creatures squirming on the bars the "masters of hanging on," but through appropriate training some of them became real gymnasts by the end of their school career. So there is nothing else for riders who have too weak abdominal muscles to do but to train.

SHOULDER-IN AND HALF PASS

We need the spiral seat in all lateral movements. In the shoulder-in, for example, we keep the seat like we had it when riding through the corner. If the rider didn't do anything differently, the horse would continue the arc through the corner into the arena. The rider prevents this by using a half halt, allowing the horse's forehand to go just as far as the inner track. The rider causes the horse to step forward and sideways with leg and rein. The rider's pelvis goes sideways and backward in the motion as it did when riding through the corner.

While riding a half pass, your instructor perhaps occasionally tells you to fix your eyes on an arrival point, toward which you should ride. The rider should reach the end of the diagonal line exactly and, in this way, keep to the prescribed path. There is more to it than that though. The rider was supposed to assume the spiral seat at the beginning of the half pass as we described in riding through the corner. When riding the half pass, this degree of turning is not enough. The turning must now come from the effort of the outer oblique abdominal muscles around the ribcage to the back and neck muscles. The rider will have the subjective feel that he will straighten himself up a little more and thereby position his outer shoulder in the direction of the horse's inner ear for the further execution of the turning. With the activation of the neck musculature, the head is turned and from the new head position, the gaze falls on the point at the end of the diagonal.

The direction to look at the arrival point serves not only for orientation. It also causes the rider to set his muscle spiral in action all the way around to its end point in the neck muscles. We have now reached a situation in which the muscle spiral is effective in its entirety. Rigidly staring down or to the other side not only hinders the neck muscles but also the function of the muscles underneath the spiral. It does not allow the spiral seat to be easy and relaxed anymore.

The leg and rein aids are described the same for the shoulder-in as for half pass in the riding manuals. Something must be pointed out here, though. In half pass, too, the rider must go in the motion of the horse, which steps with his outer legs over the inner legs in the direction of forward-sideways. In half pass right, the rider's pelvis, the right side of which is pulled forward in the spiral seat, must also go forward and sideways in the motion. The back muscles and R1 are active in this. Flexing the right rectus abdominus, i.e., bracing the back on the right side, must be avoided because this would cause the right half of the pelvis to tip back. The gluteus maximus must also not be tensed as this would prevent the forward tilting of the pelvis.

The suppleness and harmony between the horse's and rider's movements must not be disturbed, because they are of special importance in this exercise. What all must come together in riding the movement! The vertebra, which is counter-rotated to the extreme, must be balanced over a twisted pelvis, which must go in the motion of the horse forward and sideways in this position. At the same time, the lower legs must alternate and be used at the correct moment. The outside leg is used to encourage the horse's outside hind leg to cross over, and the inner works to keep the horse from dropping the inner shoulder and to maintain the forward movement. There are only a few riding exercises that are more demanding and complex in that the rider has to execute various movements at the same time.

THE TRANSITION TO CANTER

The aids to canter begin with the spiral seat, with which the rider positions his horse to the right for the right-lead canter, for example. In Müseler, we read, *If the rider were to now push the horse forward using his back and both legs combined with yielding reins, the horse would trot on positioned to the right. But in order to cause the horse to not continue to trot but instead to canter, the sequence of the steps must be changed. This happens primarily by energetically pushing the inner seat bone forward by bracing the back on one side. At the same time, both legs push the horse forward, with the inner at the girth and the outer about a hand's breadth behind the girth, but the inner leg is the main one.* What does this mean when translated into the language of the anatomy?

Let us review again. We do not push the inner seat bone forward, and we have no musculature of the back that we could brace. We use the spiral seat. For the right-lead canter, we by pull the right half of the pelvis (right hip) forward with the right inner oblique abdominal muscle. At the same time, the left outer oblique abdominal muscle and the back muscles pull the left half of the rib cage and shoulder forward. The legs take part in turning the pelvis. The outer leg now lies a little behind the girth. With the right rectus abdominus, the right half of the pelvis is pulled up in the front, whereby it lowers accordingly in the back (one-sided bracing of the back). At the same time, the riding muscles of the right pull the right lower leg to the horse's body. The right time to apply these aids is when the horse's right shoulder is going back. The aids to canter are repeated with every canter stride.

Part Three

Training

In the section about bracing the back, we traced the failure of this exercise to the fact that the students either did not know which muscles to use or that these muscles were too weak to carry out this exercise. In the first case, an explanation will suffice to cause him to use the correct muscles. In the second case, an explanation is still correct and necessary, but it will not lead to success because an explanation will not strengthen the weak muscles. Therefore, we find it advisable to make a few more remarks about the training.

For this, we must concern ourselves with the strength of the muscles and clarify a few definitions. We need this so you can understand what is to follow. In addition, these comments should give you the ability to judge for yourself which conditions and possibilities there are for your age and gender regarding the type of training and its prospects of success. Ten-year-old boys and girls have approximately the same muscle strength. As they get older, strength increases for boys quickly and reaches its peak between 20 and 30 years of age. During the course of life, this strength gradually decreases again. At 65 years of age, the remaining strength amounts to about 75 percent of the strength of a 20–30 year old. In women, the increase in strength is less and reaches about 65 percent of a man's strength between the ages of 16 and 30. The decrease in strength up to the age of 35 is about the same as for a man.

The muscle strength built by the activities of daily life, which is needed to accomplish the tasks of everyday life, is called "normal force." It will vary according to the type of activity one undertakes. A blacksmith will possess more muscle strength than a clock maker. This strength can be measured with dynamometers and instruments of more or less complexity.

One can tense every muscle over the normal amount to the fullest extent. The force that is achieved is called "maximum force."

Through appropriate training, muscles can be strengthened and their force increased. This is true up to a certain point, above which the strength cannot be increased, even with training. This condition is the "final strength" of the muscles.

Under hypnosis, muscle strength can be increased by about 10 percent. Under psychological influence, for example, in competition with the unconditional determination to win or in emergency situations, an increase in strength that exceeds what is otherwise considered to be the ultimate force under normal conditions is possible. It results in greater fatigue, however.

The length of time one can draw on the strength of the muscles is not only a question of muscle strength, but also depends on muscle circulation. A muscle is a chemically dynamic machine. A great deal of material must be transported by blood flow into the muscle cells so that it can function. For example, carbohydrates and fat are burned to produce energy. The blood also carries the oxygen that is necessary for this and carries away the byproducts of the burning process.

In dynamic work, that is, in daily life and in most sports, muscles alternate between relaxed and flexed states. Under especially good conditions, they do that in a 1:1 relationship. In moments when the muscle is relaxed, new oxygen-rich blood comes to the muscles, and the products of decomposition and products of fatigue are carried away. In this way, the continuous strength for daily life is assured. When exerting the muscles less than 15 percent of maximum force, blood circulation is always guaranteed. There is little fatigue and the strength can be maintained for an adequate length of time.

If the exertion of the muscles exceeds 20 to 30 percent of the maximum force, the blood vessels are compressed so much that no blood can flow through them. This happens especially with static muscle activity, where the muscles are continually and consistently tensed. Although this produces great force, the effect is only temporary and depends on how long the muscle can work under anaerobic conditions, i.e. with no oxygen supply. The continuous power limit value for dynamic work is twice as great as for static work. The rider who grips while riding tires more quickly because of this continual contraction of the muscles than someone who tenses the correct muscles as needed and then lets them relax again.

If the muscles are not strong enough to fulfill the demands the chosen sport places on them, they must be trained. The type of training is depends on the demands of the sport. A weight lifter and a sprinter need strong muscle packets in order to be able to achieve maximum strength exertion in a short time. The muscle exertion exceeds the critical limit of 20–30 percent of the maximum force so that the blood vessels are greatly compressed. This is acceptable in this type of sport because this great muscle exertion lasts a relatively short period of time. In the break that follows the exertion, the circulation is enough to balance out the shortage of oxygen that occurred during the phase of exertion and to carry away the waste products from the cells.

These athletes concentrate their training essentially on building muscle mass. The result is that the affected muscles can work with a small amount of contraction against a great resistance. During strength training, also called isometric training, the exertion of the muscles results in a thickening of the individual muscle fibers if muscle length remains the same. With continued training, the number of muscle fibers increases. The blood vessels also expand in the process, but this remains inconsequential compared to the increase in muscle substance. It is also of secondary importance in these types of sports.

It is different for long distance runners. He only needs a fraction of the muscle exertion of a weight lifter or a sprinter, but he has to do it for a long time. For him, strength is less important than muscle stamina. In order to develop it, he needs a type of training that increases the circulation. He achieves this with isotonic training, by which the muscle changes its length with consistent exertion. While isometric training strength is built by the contractions of a few muscles working against a great resistance, isotonic training endurance is achieved by many contractions working against a small resistance. The result is less muscle mass, but the blood vessels expand. When the long distance runner succeeds in running with relaxed muscles, which keeps the exertion under the critical limit of 20–30 percent of the maximum force, he can keep it up with increased circulation ratios for a relatively long period of time.

Strength and stamina training cannot replace each other. They must be implemented according to the desired type of sport. They must be trained separately but used together as needed.

In addition to the increase in muscle mass and the expansion of the blood vessels, muscle exertion works like a pump on the entire heart and circulatory system and strengthens them. It also positively affects the elasticity of the ligament apparatus of the joint, and the ability of the nerves to react, which provides for the cooperation of the muscles.

To be successful, the muscle training must demand more than what is demanded of the muscles in daily life or what is presently demanded in any sporting activity. The training requirements must be continuously increased if they are to remain a training stimulus for a longer period of time. However, you should not train until you are completely exhausted because it decreases the training effect. Trainers and experienced athletes know this and proceed accordingly.

If different muscle groups are trained at the same time, success does not have to appear in all groups simultaneously. The available starting strength of the individual muscles plays a role at the beginning of training. Someone with abdominal muscles of average strength will reach the maximum strength through training faster than someone who has completely weak abdominal muscles. If a person has strong leg muscles he will progress with these more quickly. In general, the effect of training during the first few weeks is minimal. Training periods of 10–12 weeks will be necessary to reach the targeted maximum strength for individual muscle groups.

When training stops, the additional strength that was gained is gradually lost. The normal strength remains, which is increased according to the regular athletic use of the musculature. While the normal strength remains pretty stable throughout life, the strength gained through training must always be maintained by repeated training periods.

When a limb is immobilized after it has been broken, for example, the muscle strength is lost quickly and to a great extent. This happens to trained muscles to a greater degree than to those that are subjected to only normal daily demands. Many weeks of training are required to regain the old strength.

The body is better able to train in the morning than in the afternoon or in the evening because of the positive effects of an increased vitamin supply and ultraviolet light. This also explains the seasonal variations of performance capability, the optimum of which is in autumn. An increase in performance cannot be achieved by increasing vitamin intake. We will not go into other possibilities of influencing it by taking drugs and doping up, because we reject such measures. One does not become a Grand Prix rider by taking medically prescribed pills, but rather through hard work using the talent available and the appropriate horse.

The trainability of individual people varies greatly. It is generally less for women than for men. In youth, it is about the same for boys and girls. With age, it increases greatly for boys and reaches its peak for men between the ages of 20 and 30. In women between the ages of 20 and 30, it comprises only about 50 percent of that of men in that age group. With increased age, this difference between the sexes decreases.

Predicting who is trainable and who is less trainable cannot be done. Some individuals are very trainable and become top athletes. For others, success remains small despite intensive training. Only through a practical training trial of at least six weeks can the trainability of a person be determined.

For every type of sport, a general endurance training is recommended as a foundation. It must be especially solid if you want to participate in competitive sports. To achieve this, you will have to put together a program yourself that, for example, can have basic gymnastics as a foundation: head rolls, bending the hips forward, sideways and backward; turning the hips, turning the hips in circles, deep knee bends and push-ups. Jumping rope and running can also be added.

If especially important muscle groups for the intended type of sport are too weak, they must be developed through a separate, targeted training program. From what we learned in the previous chapters, we know that the dressage rider must constantly use the muscles of the anterior side of the abdominal wall and the riding muscles of the upper leg in order to fulfill the basic requirements of the dressage—bracing the back, going in the motion of the horse and half halting, for example. According to our observations, these two muscle groups are too weak for the demands of dressage in most people who start riding. Due to a lack of knowledge, they are still too weak in many who have ridden for a long time because they have never been correctly used to stretch the spine and turn the hips.

This muscle group must have targeted strength training. We recommend "isometric muscle training," as described by Hettinger. (Editor's Note: this refers to *Isometrishes Muskeltraining*, which has never been published in English. We recommend *The New Total Rider* by Tom Holmes, and *Fit for Riding* by Eckart Meyners. Both are published by Half Halt Press, Inc.). The method is so simple that even those working full time can do it several times a day without difficulty. It promises results if done regularly and systematically.

As we have described earlier with strength training, we proceed from the recognition that a few muscle flexions against a great resistance increases the strength of the muscles, which increases muscle mass. These muscle groups need to be exerted to the maximum three to five times a day.

We would like to recommend a few exercises for this, which we will explain with some short text and appropriate pictures.

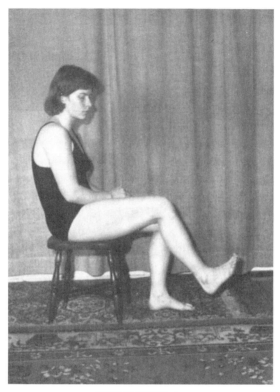

EXERCISE 1

1. For the extensor, or stretching, muscles on the front of the lower leg: Pull the toes forward and up and hold this position of maximum flexion for about five seconds (count slowly to five).

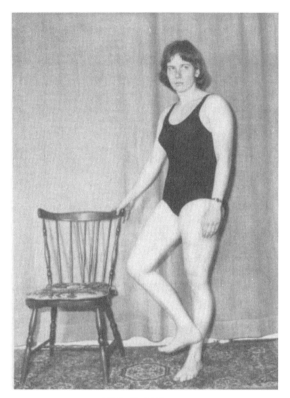

EXERCISE 2

2. For the riding muscles of the thigh: while standing on one leg (for safety, hold on to a chair with one hand) place the lower third of the rear side of the lower leg one-third of the way up in front of the front of the other lower leg. From this position, try to bend the leg at the knee by pushing with all your strength against the resistance of the leg upon which you are standing. Hold for five seconds. With the other hand, you will be able to feel the tensed riding muscles R2 through R4 on the back side of the thigh and from underneath the iliac spine R1.

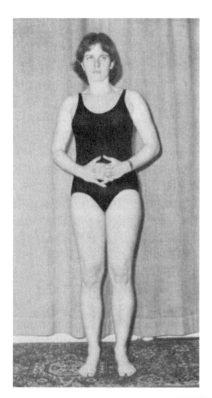 

EXERCISE 3

3. For the abdominal muscles (exercise recommended by Hettinger): Cross your arms in front of your belly and pull the arms back. Tense the abdominal muscles to the maximum and hold. Again, as in the previous exercises and also in the following, hold for about five seconds. An alternative: Grab the ends of a towel placed across your back and pull forward strongly. Tense the abdominal muscles to resist it.

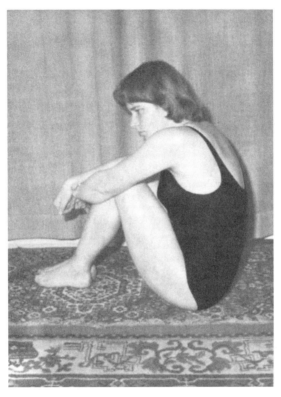

EXERCISE 4

4. For the back muscles (an exercise recommended by Hettinger): While sitting on the floor, pull the knees to the upper body as far as possible. Place your arms so that your elbows are around your lower legs. Straighten your upper body against the resistance of the arms.

EXERCISE 5

5. For both abdominal and back muscles: While standing, stretch the spine as much as possible. At the same time, tense the abdominal muscles on both sides as much as possible and pull your pelvis forward and up, and tip it to the rear.

EXERCISE 6

6. For the abdominal, back and riding muscles: Begin as in exercise 2. Pull one side of the pelvis forward and up, and at the same time, tip it backward with the right and then left abdominal muscles. Stretch the spine up at the same time. Pay attention that the knees move to the outside and not to the inside so that the "grippers" are not used.

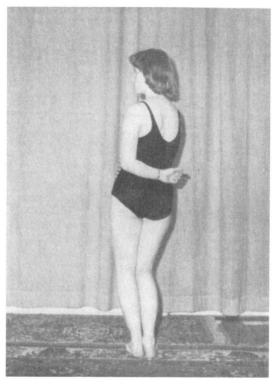

EXERCISE 7

7. For the combination of abdominal and back muscles used to turn the hips: Begin by standing with slightly bent knees. Bend the right arm at the elbow to about a 90 degree angle, so that the underarm lies over the breast, and place the left arm in the same position across the back. Pull the left hip and the right half of the rib cage forward toward each other. The hands should move in opposite directions. As usual, hold for five seconds at maximum flexion, then switch.

8.   Or, turn as in Exercise 7. Straighten the spine and, at the same time, pull the forward half of the pelvis up (use rectus abdominus muscle).

9.   Turning as in Exercise 7. From this position, tip the pelvic half that has been pulled forward on one side of the hips sideways using the abdominal muscles. Finish by doing the exercise in the other direction.

Every employed person, even those under the most time pressure, can use this training method, which takes no more than 15 minutes from the day. You can train your abdominal muscles while sitting at a desk without anyone noticing. You can also stand up and do the other exercises while working at your desk, which is motivating, relaxing and refreshing all at the same time.

It is, of course, up to the individual to also train isotonically. Keeping the importance of the abdominal muscles in mind, for example, you can cross the hands behind your head and lift yourself from the lying to the sitting position using your abdominal muscles each morning before getting up. You would then lie down again and repeat it. Depending on the strength of the muscles, at first this will be possible perhaps only three or four times, but eventually 10 times or more could be possible. In this way, everyone has the possibility of training either his muscle strength or stamina separately or at the same time, for the body in general or for targeted muscle groups.

PART FOUR

Teaching and Learning

For this chapter, let's return to Müseler's manual and excerpt from it the following statement, *Correctly ridden horses are as seldom found as really good riders. In addition, 99 percent of all riders cannot go in the motion of the horse or stick to the saddle, because they have not learned to brace the back.*

What every child can do on a swing is too hard for most riders to attempt. Every rider should think about whether or not he should try to master this dark secret for himself.

We read here again that bracing the back and going in the horse's motion are just as important in riding as is adding one and one for counting and the continued mathematical training of a student.

Now judge for yourself how far you have come after years of effort in the saddle to acquire the basics of riding. Do you belong to that one percent of select riders who have the prospect of becoming the riding equivalent of high school students or, in certain cases, to even reach the riding equivalent of college? The one who can assert that he has achieved this will be happy, but it is depressing for those who must admit they have not mastered the bracing of the back and going in the horse's motion to which supposedly 99 percent of all riders belong. None of them have mastered the basics of riding and remain the riding equivalents of remedial school children.

And how do riding instructors feel about these numbers? Are they happy or are they depressed? At first, one may think they would be happy because they have mastered the basics of bracing the back. This feeling of happiness regarding one's own riding ability should be juxtaposed against the satisfaction of their career and professional reputation, which depends essentially on the success of their instruction. If Müseler's numbers are still correct today, a one percent success must be depressing for instructors.

From our own experience and that of others, we all know that enormous difficulties are encountered when trying to analyze failing students. From the instructor's perspective, one makes it too easy for himself if the failure is attributed to the student's insufficient talent alone, or conversely, from the student's or parent's perspective, the cause of the problem is attributed to the instructor alone.

There were times in schools (but not only in schools) that authoritarian educational methods were used. This was supposedly bad and anti-authoritative teaching methods began to be taught. The result was that it went from bad to worse. Here and there, serious doubts are being expressed and people are talking about a new way, an education of partnership. This is not the place to talk about school reform, but a partnership between riding instructor and riding student may be necessary and purposeful because the required tasks are considerable.

Let us assume that Müseler is correct in his opinion that 99 percent of all riders are not able to learn what every child can do on a swing, i.e., to brace the back. One could infer that he considered 99 percent of all riders to be too dumb and too untalented to master such a childish task. Riding instructor arrogance? No, we do not think so. He certainly did not want to express such a negative blanket judgment. Rather, he 1. wanted to emphasize the importance of bracing the back in dressage riding. And 2., he wanted to prompt people to think about the fact that the process of bracing the back is nothing other than what every child on a swing does. 3. He wanted to give helpful advice as to how to learn the bracing of the back by giving readers a word picture. However, we have our doubts about that image.

There are swings that are so stable that even an adult can sit on them. One could think about having the following competition with two swings. On the first swing, a child would be allowed to move the swing and to stop it in the conventional and usual way. On the second swing, one of the best dressage riders would be allowed to move the swing and to stop it but only by bracing the back. The child would certainly win this competition. After a short time, the child would swing forward and backward to great heights, while the dressage rider would have to be satisfied with moving his swing very little.

The reason for this is that the child pushes off. While the swing goes forward, the upper body leans back and pushes the lower legs forward and up at the same time. When the swing goes back, the upper body goes forward and the lower legs are bent back, in order to repeat the process when the swing reaches its maximum backward-swinging point. In contrast, the dressage rider must keep his upper body straight and quiet, and his legs must hang down loosely. Tipping the pelvis alone would not be enough to cause the swing to move very much. The dressage rider has certainly achieved great victories as a Grand Prix rider, but on the swing will just as certainly be the big loser. Bracing the back alone will not be enough on the swing.

It is, therefore, not child's play for the rider to learn the bracing of the back, nor is it child's play for the riding instructor to explain to the rider how he should do that. The reference to the swing is also not that helpful because the assumptions and methods are too different. The other exercises recommended by Müseler to learn the bracing of the back are only partially correct and to a limited extent, because he could not proceed from the correct conditions due to a lack of anatomical knowledge. He certainly would have suggested other exercises that used the correct muscles if they had been at his disposal.

We gladly met Müseler's demands of thinking about the secret of bracing the back. By providing you with anatomical knowledge, we have tried to make the necessary movements more intelligible. Now the rider can determine which of his muscles he needs to train in a targeted manner. With this knowledge, the instructor is better able to explain, which makes the instruction easier, and the student is better able to understand and learn what is taught.

If the teacher can explain to the student that to brace the back, he must pull the front edge of his pelvis up with the abdominal muscles so that the back part of his pelvis tips to the rear along with the sacrum, and if the teacher can make that clear to the student through additional illustrations, the student would certainly be able to understand and learn it more easily. We can certainly assume that considerably more than one percent of all riders are physically and mentally able to understand this and carry it out.

In many cases, as previously mentioned, the chair seat is the greatest annoyance to riding students and instructors alike. In every riding lesson, there is always the same command, "Bring your legs back!" It continues for weeks and months. For some it never stops. The student becomes sad and disappointed because of his ineptitude. The instructor comes to the resigned conclusion, "There is no point, he will never learn it." But maybe the student would understand it more easily and learn it more quickly if one would explain to him that the cause of his legs being too far forward is not his legs, but rather the position and tilting of his pelvis, which is tipped too far to the rear. This is easy to do with an illustration and can be easily tried and systematically practiced on a horse with a quiet gait. The evil chair seat would be ripped out by the roots. It may be possible to do away with it even in the so-called hopeless cases.

The riders who use the incorrect trot seat as described on pages 80–87 cannot go with the horse's motion. They have never noticed that one can tip the pelvis to the side and can also turn it. This mistaken behavior is so noticeable and easy to see that no instructor should miss it. With the possibility of explaining it, there should also be the possibility of remedying it and teaching the student the correct use of the muscles to move correctly with the horse's motion. As we showed on page 69, the rider who cannot go in the motion of the horse will also have problems with the half halt, and so a vicious circle of mistakes develops. Would this be prevented if going in the motion of the horse were systematically taught and learned from the beginning and the half halt developed from that?

In the riding texts, there is much written and in great detail about correcting incorrectly trained horses. One finds nothing about correcting incorrectly trained riders. Probably there would be a lot fewer ill-trained horses if there were fewer ill-trained riders. Perhaps this vicious circle would be broken by correct training and learning.

Let's address Steinbrecht's opinion that both half halting and bracing the back are purely matters of feel. According to him, the rider who does not have this feel can never learn it because it is not something that can be taught. This could be something like a blank check to excuse those who are reluctant or unable to teach. The number of these people is undoubtedly small, but which profession has no black sheep? They could make use of this opinion as necessary, which is not meaningless due to Steinbrecht's authority.

Steinbrecht's opinion that feel is not very teachable stems from his insufficient ability to explain it. One can neither explain something, nor teach it, if it uses muscles one does not know about. What else is left than to make the entire issue purely a matter of feel? From every line of Steinbrecht's book we have the impression that he was not only a very good rider, but that he was just as good and as passionate an instructor. He would have been ready to explain what he considered to be a matter of feel if he'd had the tools for that. The knowledge-hungry student has the right to ask, "How does one do that?" The instructor who is willing to teach will only answer with much frustration, "That is a matter of feel. Either you have it or you will never learn it." Surely the instructor would prefer to use the tools that the basics of anatomy offer to explain and teach the movements in riding. In most other sports, it is commonplace to instruct according to this foundation.

Let us get back to gripping with the thighs. What help to the student is the command, "Don't grip," if no one tells him what he should do instead to hold himself on the horse, and if no one explains it to him, which muscles should he use and which should he not use? When generations of riding instructors have told their students to brace the small of the back, which does not even exist, they are beyond our reproach because they could not have known better. Originally, the assumption was that the leg was moved by the leg musculature the same way the arm was moved by the arm musculature. Thus, the small of the back must have been moved by muscles in the surrounding area. This assumption was then passed on as fact. But if the student learns right from the start how to correctly use his muscles, he will not even begin gripping.

On page 83, we promised to come back to this problem because it's so important to avoid gripping. In addition, we ask you to join us into the medical area, this time, into neurology. We must ask the doctors among our readers for understanding if we do not go too deeply into this topic to allow for understanding of the laypeople who read this book. We want not only to explain the unpleasant function of gripping by discussing the nerves, but also to primarily explain how to overcome it. From this, essential tips for the instruction and learning can be derived. We identified gripping as a natural and useful reflex action (page 82), which the body uses to protect itself from the unpleasant effects on the seat.

The irritation that the pressure on the saddle and the motion of the horse cause on the perineum and the legs is conducted through the nerve pathways to the spinal cord. There it is redirected in the reflex center to other nerve pathways, which lead to the gripping muscles and cause them to contract. The entire process takes place quickly and without the brain's participation or our willing it to happen. Figure 44 illustrates the reflex cycle.

The spinal cord makes up only a part of the entire central nervous system. It does serves not only the reflex actions just described. Also running through it are pathways, which direct sense stimuli past the reflex center of the spinal cord to the higher centers of the brain stem and the cortex. Other pathways, the motor pathways, lead from there back to the muscles (Figure 44).

A vast number of stimuli and irritations from the skin, muscles and joints and, above all, from the sense organs, travel the sensory pathways through many nerve centers to the cortex where they are processed into conscious sensations and perceptions. From the great number of stimuli, the automatic filter of the brain is only aware of as many as is required by the body. The selection that is made by the brain is always optimal.

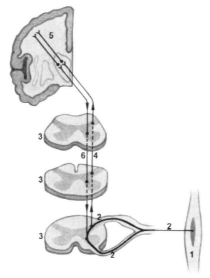

FIGURE 44. Reflex Arc and Nerve Pathways of the Brain

1. muscle; 2. reflex arc; 3. spinal cord; 4. sensory pathway to the brain; 5. brain; 6. motor pathway from the brain

In different places in the brain, the response to each stimulus is formed and sent back to the periphery. Motor function, which is an activity of the muscles, is also dependent on the higher brain centers working together. They make voluntary movements possible. If I will to grasp something, to brace my back or to use my lower legs, they convert this desire to reality. The motor structures of the brain serve primarily to coordinate the individual motor components such as tipping the pelvis, bending the lower legs, the opposite turning of the shoulders and hips, and half halts. If the rider wants to use the spiral seat, he does not need to think about if, when and how strongly he should first use the left rectus abdominus, then the left inner oblique abdominal muscle, then the right outer oblique abdominal muscle, and finally the back and neck muscles to a greater or lesser extent. His excellent brain takes care of all of this for him if he knows which body part he wants to move, with which muscle, and in which direction.

As a rider, it boils down to not having to let everything happen automatically, such as when gripping. The reflex paths only go to the spinal cord and function without the brain's involvement. Instead, I must come up with a procedure that is consciously directed by my brain and remains subject to my will. It will not do to mechanically, reflexively and automatically grip. It would be much better to purposefully and consciously use the abdominal muscles to influence the back, to consciously go with the horse's motion by using alternating back muscles and riding muscles of the thigh, and to implement the spiral seat by using the abdominal and back muscles, etc.

How does this happen? If I have carried out a desired exercise once correctly, for example, using the riding muscles of the upper thigh to operate my legs, muscle memory is stored in the various centers of the nervous system. This allows the stimulus that took place to be recalled. Those motor nerve patterns that are especially important for achieving a particular part of the exercise are selectively tracked. The co-activation of other motor and sensory systems that originally occurred is kept to a minimum. In this way, the entire process takes place faster the more it is repeated. The special nerve patterns that develop through constant repetition of movement combinations are stored in a section of the central nervous system and form the foundation for the eventual automation of movement. Instead of the mechanical reflex that automatically runs along the spinal cord and results in the use of the grippers, an automatic use of the riding muscles of the thighs develops in the brain that is subject to the rider's will.

We conclude that a student must experience which muscles to use during the individual exercises from the beginning so that the individual exercises are correctly programmed by his central nervous system. Through frequent repetition, they can eventually become the desired automatic actions. If the use of incorrect muscles was programmed and, therefore, the exercise in question is done incorrectly, it will be very difficult to turn an incorrect automatic movement into a correct one.

If we had wanted to avoid a neurological explanation, we could have just said, "Practice with the correct muscles until it is second nature." If we, however, want to make this popular saying closer to the neurological reality, we would say, "until it is second nature for the muscles and brain."

This is not a process that can be achieved quickly. It is important for the rider to have information about the movements of individual riding exercises and about the necessary muscle use for these. The indication that frequent repetitions are necessary brings up the question of whether or not some exercises should be systematically practiced and drilled in order to ensure the correct execution by using the correct muscles, for example, the use of the lower legs, straightening the spine, going with the motion, counter-rotation of the spine, etc. Drill-like practice methods are not very popular today and are rejected to a great degree as antiquated methods. The neurological perspective may have shown, however, that drill-like repetitions still have basic value today, because they are required by our central nervous system.

We do not consider it to be our task to develop a new riding system. Riding instructors understand more about that than we do. We consider it advisable, however, to point out that knowledge of the anatomy and the conclusions that are to be drawn from it can be used to develop teaching methods that expand and facilitate the teaching and learning of dressage. On the other hand, it also lets us test the common teaching methods for their usefulness and effectiveness, both for the long-term riding instruction as well as for individual riding lessons. If one thinks critically, doubts could creep in here and there about whether the old, solidly entrenched teaching methods are still the best today.

Steinbrecht was certainly correct when he said that long-winded explanations are not possible during the course of a practical riding lesson. The action is too fast; even a short explanation by the instructor is always much longer than the exercise to be performed. One must conclude that the necessary explanations must be given before the riding lesson.

The student who has received an explanation about what is to be practiced in the lesson and told which muscles he should use to master the exercise will notice what he did wrong in the practical riding lesson with only a short correction by the instructor. It will be easier for him to correct his mistake.

This demands patience from the instructor and the student. Individuals need varying amounts of time to succeed in using the correct muscles for the desired purpose and to practice correctly until it becomes automatic. The instructor will be able to tell where the necessary muscle strength is lacking. He can recommend additional muscle training before the student slips into using the wrong muscles.

Further patience is required because the level of training and the different kinds of horses are difficult to ascertain. We also have to keep in mind that the horse is a living creature and has its own will. It must also be trained for the exercise that it is supposed to perform. The blood, muscles, tendons, bones and nerves play a significant role for the horse as well. The horse will react differently to different riders. It will be subject to external influences just as the rider is and will tire just as easily. One must not make excessive demands or make it fatigued. A break at the appropriate time is helpful, and can be used for additional explanations. Most riders today are "desk jockeys" with few physical demands. Therefore, it is not helpful to chase these students around the arena for an hour according to the motto, "What does not kill us will make us stronger." The result is that the correct muscles tire quickly and the body reverts back to using protective automatic reflexes. The attempt to reach a desired strength results in nothing more than strengthening the old mistakes: gripping, rigid pelvis and the chair seat.

Now there is a point beyond which it is not possible for the instructor to recognize the cause of small mistakes made by the rider. When executing a halt, for example, the student should tip the pelvis by using the abdominal muscles. He should also use the lower legs by means of the riding muscles of the thigh. Even experienced riders must admit, if they watch themselves closely, that the thighs grip the saddle briefly, especially when halting from a fast gait. The riding instructor will not be able to see it unless it occurs to a great extent. He will be able to tell that the halt was not correct, however, which he will be able to point out to the student. The student will figure out by himself that he used the grippers again.

Let us look at the half pass exercise. The rider has made practical progress over a period of time. He has practiced in peace, gradually corrected mistakes according to the corrections of his instructor. Today, however, he cannot execute the movement fluently. The instructor sees this but cannot determine the cause despite careful observation and consideration. He finally expresses his dissatisfaction by saying, "The brakes are on somewhere." Suddenly the rider remembers the possible places where the brakes can be put on, which he has heard about often enough in the theoretical instruction. Examples of this are tightening the grippers, incorrect tilting of the pelvis, tensing the hip joint ligament, not going with the motion enough, not twisting the spine enough. Just as quickly, he realizes that he concentrated too much on using the outer leg today and clamped the outside leg on the horse too much at times. This prevented the pelvis from being able to go in the motion enough. The well-trained horse notices this and reacts to it. The instructor saw that there was a problem, but even the best instructor would be unable to tell in the few seconds it takes for a movement to be performed where the cause of a problem lies. This is unless the mistake is so obvious that the entire exercise is a failure.

Only the rider can tell where the "brake" was on. The instructor's remark was enough to wake him up, make him analyze his position, make him aware of the mistake and to let him consciously correct the mistake. The previous instruction and practice allowed the rider to be able to feel the mistake and to correct it even in a situation where the instructor could not pinpoint the small mistake exactly and give only a general comment. His instructor helped him help himself. The student knows he will always need this help. The feel the rider develops in this way is an acquired, taught, consciously willed and consciously learned feel. It will not be left to chance so that one of a hundred riders, by coincidence, is bestowed this feel as a gift by the grace of fate.

The instructor plays a part in determining the pace of training depending on the progress of the rider. Plagued by differing ambitions, the students often want more than they are capable of. One wants to shine at shows. Who is free of vanity? One wants to ride Fourth Level movements before one has mastered Second Level movements and still has problems with them because the basics such as half halting and going with the horse's motion are still lacking. One wants to do higher multiplication even though one still cannot do lower multiplication correctly. It is good that there is no set theory for riding. In these cases, the instructor should point out the limits clearly and critically, but should also offer the rider the possibility of expanding the limits through appropriate instruction. The rider should bring his excessive ambition in line with his ability. Even this partnership has to be practiced. Openness and honesty form the best foundation for every type of partnership.

In many cases, the instructor is also training the horse that his student rides. In general, it is proper for the beginner to buy an older horse with the instructor's help, a horse that is quiet and allows him to learn the basic seat. In Steinbrecht we read that the old masters put their students on horses performing piaffe in the pillars to teach them how to go with the horse's motion. That was certainly ideal, but it is hardly possible today.

If I explain to a rider of average talent how to go with the horse's motion, he can learn it on any horse. He will have to work at this, because he does not want to make slower progress in his training than his horse.

The partnership between the instructor and the rider becomes a partnership of three, because the training of the horse has been added. This relationship should function for all three. A well-trained horse makes learning easier for the student and increases his enjoyment of riding. A well-trained rider makes it easier for the instructor to keep the horse in the appropriate training condition or to even advance his training. Both increase the professional success of the riding instructor and his professional reputation. It plays a part in improving what Müseler considers to be the depressing success ratio of his teaching of 99 to one.

Everything taken together should lead to what Müseler desires, that the bracing of the back, going with the horse's motion and riding dressage will no longer remain a "dark secret." Even Bürger says the upper regions of dressage border on magic.

Magic tricks are only worth something as long as you do not know the tricks the magician is using. If the spectators figure out how he does it, then his show is worthless.

Dressage riding is, thank God, not magic. Because of this, one can in good conscious not only ask, "How do I do that?" but also one must give his all to answer this question. With the answer, a cheap magic trick that would make dressage riding worthless and uninteresting is not revealed. The answer solidifies and expands the starting point of a sport that is unequalled in its life-affirming, educational, and aesthetic value and, with increasing perfection, can be magically beautiful.

BIBLIOGRAPHY

Braus, Hermann. *Anatomie des Mensche* (Human Anatomy).Expanded by Curt Elze. Berln–Göttingen–Heidelberg: Springer-Verlag, 1954.

Bürger, Udo. *Vollendete Reitkunst* (The Perfection of the Art of Riding). 4th Edition. Berlin and Hamburg: Verlag Paul Parey, 1975.

Fick, Rudolf. *Handbuch der Anatomie und Mechanik der Gelenke* (Handbook of Anatomy and Joint Mechanics). Part 3: Spezielle Gelenk- und Muskelmechanik (Special Mechanics of Joints and Muscles). Jena: Verlag Gustav Fischer, 1911.

Hettinger, Theodor. *Isometrisches Muskeltraining* (Isometric Muscle Training). 4th Edition. Stuttgart: Verlag Georg Thieme, 1972.

Janzen, Rudolf. *Elemente der Neurologie* (Elements of Neurology). Berlin–Heidelberg–New York: Springer-Verlag, 1972.

Keidel, Wolf D. *Lehrbuch der Physiologie* (Study of Physiology). 2nd Revised Edition. Stuttgart: Verlag Geor Thieme, 1970.

Müseler, Wilhelm. *Reitlehre* (Riding Logic). 43rd Edition. Berlin and Hamburg: Verlag Paul Parey, 1978.

Podhajsky, Alois. *Die klassische Reitkunst* (The Classical Art of Riding). 2nd Edition. Munich: Nymphenburger Verlagshandlung, 1965.

Rauber, August, and Friedrich Kopsch *Lehrbuch und Atlas der Anatomie des Menschen* (Study and Atlas of Human Anatomy). Revised by Gian Töndury. Volume 1: *Bewegungsapparat* (Movement Apparatus). Stuttgart: Verlag Georg Thieme, 1968.

Seeger, Louis. *System der Reitkunst* (System of Riding).
    Hildesheim - New York: Olms Presse, 1974.
Sobotta, Johannes, and Hellmuth Becher. *Atlas der Anatomie*
    des Menschen (Atlas of Human Anatomy). Part 1.
    Munich - Berlin - Vienna: Urban und Schwarzenberg,
    1967.
Steinbrecht, Gustav. *Gymnasium des Pferdes* (Gymnasium of
    the Horse). 6th Edition. Aachen: Verlag Dr. Rudolf
    Georgi, 1969.
Wätjen, Richard. *Dressurreiten* (Dressage). 8th Edition. Berlin
    and Hamburg: Verlag Paul Parey, 1978.

ILLUSTRATIONS

Müseler, Wilhelm. *Reitlehre* (Riding Logic). 31st, 32nd
Editions. Berlin and Hamburg: Verlag Paul Parey, 1978.
Figures 42 and 43.

Müseler, Wilhelm. *Reitlehre* (Riding Logic). 43rd
Edition. Berlin and Hamburg: Verlag Paul Parey, 1978.

Figures 25, 26, 27, and 32. Werner Menzendorf).

Willers, Gisela. Photos for Excercises 1–7.

The drawings, with the exception of Figure 32, with
thanks to Mr. Roland Helmus, Hamburg.

Index

Illustrations are in italics

Abdominal muscles, *41, 42*
   exercises for, 116, 118, 199
   importance of, 94-95
   in bracing the back, 60, 62
   in full halts and half halts, 70,
   72
   in going with the motion of
   the horse, 62-63
   in riding through the corner,
   58, 80, 82, 84, 97, 99-100
   in spiral seat, 89, 93, 94
Adductors, *See also* Grippers,
36, 38-39, *34, 35, 37*

Back, *See also* Bracing the back
   and Spine, 49, 51, 52, 54, 58,
   60, 61, 66, 69, 70, 71, 91, *42,*
   85, 92, 96
   exercises for, 117, 118, 199,
   120
   hollow, 83-87
   in full halts and half halts, 73
   in shoulder-in and half pass
   100-101
   muscles of 42-42, 79, 93, 95,
   100, *100,* 132, 133
Balance, 65, 8
   in going with the motion of
   the horse, 74-80
   losing, 60
Bones, *See also* individual
   bones, 15-31
Bracing the back, 47, 48-53, 62,
   63-64, 67, 84, 85, 94, 101,
   102, 107, 113, 125, 126, 127,
   128, 129
Bürger, Udo, 9, 69, 139, 141

Canter, 64, 69, 98, *97*
   transition to, 57, 102-103
Center of gravity, 76, 77, 78, 80,
   94, 98, *76, 77*
Chair seat, 31, 83-85, 86, 128,
   136
   Driving, 58, 62, 72, *72*

Exercises, 113-121
   isometric, 108, 110, 113, 140,
   isotonic, 110

Foot, 39, 47, 54, 55, 56, 58, 98

Going with the motion of the
   horse, 58-66, 72, 74-8

Grippers, *See also* Adductors,
   38-39, 54, 55, 60, 68, 69, 80,
   81, 82, 87, 133, 136, 137,
   119, *34, 35, 37*

Half pass, 95, 100-102, 136
Halts, full and half, 66-73, *67, 68,*
   70
   half halt, 98, 100, 112, 113,
   128, 132, 136
Heel, 39, 40, 55, 56, 78, *38*
Hip joint ligament, 27-31, *28, 29,*
   30
   in halts, 69
   in the chair seat, 83-84
   in the hollow back, 86
Hollow back, 85-87

Iliac crest, 20, 28, 40, 52, *20, 40,*
   52
Ilium, 31, *20, 21*
Ischial ramus, 20, 25, 99, *20, 23*
Ischial tuberosity, 20, *20, 21, 23*
   28, 29, 34, 36, 57, 96

Knee, 31, 33, 34, 35, 36, 38, 54,
   55, 56, 58, 61, 63, 65, 67,
   80, 112, *22, 34, 35, 39, 61,*
   62, 67, 70, 72

Lateral movements, 50, 88, 93,
   98
   shoulder-in and half pass,
   100-102
Leg, *See also* Lower leg, 27-29,
   31, 59, 60, 75, 84, 88, 90, 99,
   112, 128, 130
   in full halts and half halts, 67,
   69-71, 72, 73
   in shoulder-in and half pass,
   100-101
   in transition to canter
   muscles of, 33-40
   using the, 54-58
Ligament, hip joint,
   exercise, effect on, 110
Lower leg, 34, 36, 38-40, 60-61,
   63-70, *72, 82,* 95, 98, 115,
   132, 134, 136, *34, 36, 38, 39,*
   57, 96
   exercises for, 114,
   in chair seat, 83,
   muscles of, 34, 36, 38-40,
   using the, 54-58, 60

Maximum strength, 109, 111
Muscles. See also muscle
   groups, i.e. seat, thigh, back,
   etc.17, 32-43,
   abdominal, 40-42
   back, 42-43
   thigh and lower legs, 33-40
   seat, 32-33
Müseler, Wilhelm, 7, 9, 45, 48,
   49, 50, 51, 52, 60, 61, 66, 68,
   69, 70, 78, 84, 86, 88, 96,
   102, 123, 125, 126, 127, 128,
   136, 141, 142

Neurology, 130-134

Pelvic ring, 20, 23, 24
Pelvis, 19-27, 28, 29, 31, 32, 33,
   35, 36, 37, 38, 40, 42, 47, 54,
   80, 82, 83, 103, 118, 119,
   120, 128, 136, 137, 20, 21,
   23, 24, 25, 30, 67, 76, 84, 96
   in bracing the lower back, 48,
   49, 50, 51, 52
   in chair seat, 84, 85, 86
   in full and half halts, 67, 69,
   70, 71, 72, 74, 76, 77, 78
   in going with the motion of the
   horse, 58, 59, 60, 61, 63, 64,
   65, 66
   in shoulder-in and half pass,
   100-102
   in spiral seat 87, 90, 94, 95
   tipping the, 58, 84, 86, 126,
   129, 132, 136
Podhajsky, Alois, 9, 69, 141
Pubic crest, 20, 23, 20, 35, 41,
   42
Pubic ramus, 20, 25, 31, 38, 47,
   81, 84, 99, 20, 21, 28, 29, 36,
   37, 57, 96

Rectus abdominus, 49, 90, 92,
   121, 42
Riding Logic, ("riding manual"), 7,
   8, 45, 52, 60, 79, 140

Sacrum, 23-24, 48-51, 59, 65, 74,
   79, 86, 128, 18, 20, 23, 61,
   62, 67, 70, 72, 75
Sartorius, 33, 35, 57, 96
Seat, 24, 38, 49, 78, 82, 87, 131,
   32
   chair, 83-85, 86, 128, 136
   foundation of, 26-31
   incorrect, 64, 80, 127
   in going with the motion of
   the horse, 60, 61, 63, 127

muscles of, 32-33, 54
   points of support for, 47
   spiral, 87-97, 98-102, 132-
   133
Seeger, Louis, 69, 142
Shoulder-in, 100-102
Spine, 15-19, 16, 17, 18
   back muscles and stabilization
   of, 42
   in balance, 74-75, 78-80
   in bracing the back, 48-49,
   51
   in going with the horse's
   motion, 64-66
   in spiral seat, 94
   stretching of the, 65, 67, 70,
   73, 79, 80
Spiral seat (turning seat), 78, 87-
   97, 132, 92, 97
   in riding through the corner,
   98-99
   in shoulder-in and half pass,
   100-101
   in transition to canter, 102
Steinbrecht, Gustav, 9, 69, 70,
   88, 93, 95, 96, 128, 129, 130,
   135, 138, 142
Strength training. See also
   Isometric exercises, 108 112
Suppleness, 80, 101
   and gripping, 80-83

Thigh, 40, 54, 55, 56, 58, 60, 61,
   66, 68, 87, 88, 95, 133, 22,
   28, 29, 30, 34, 35, 36, 39, 61,
   62, 67, 70, 85, 96
   bone, 19, 21, 29, 31
   exercise for, 115
   gripping with, 69, 80-81, 82,
   130
   in full and half halts, 69, 72
   in going with the motion of the
   horse, 72
   in hollow back, 86,
   in riding through corners, 99
   in spiral seat, 89, 90-91, 95,
   136
   in transition to canter, 103
   muscles, 33-38, 39, 61, 62, 67
Training. See also Strength train-
   ing105-121

Vertebrae. See also Spine, 15-19,
   16, 17, 18, 23

Wätjen, Richard, 9, 88, 142